What Is The Purpose of Marriage?

Mary Esanbor

Library of Congress Control Number: 2010917965

ISBN:	Hardcover	978-1-4568-0698-9
	Softcover	978-1-4568-0697-2
	Ebook	978-1-4568-0699-6

This book was printed in the United States of America.

To order additional copies of this book, contact:
Xlibris Corporation
0-800-644-6988
www.xlibrispublishing.co.uk
Orders@Xlibrispublishing.co.uk
301103

Contents

Acknowledgements

I am grateful to my husband, Christian Osamwonyi Esanbor, for his patients and support during my late-night writings and his suggestions and advice. 'Thank you, honey.'

To my five children: Florence, Prince, Jacqueline, Joshua, and Angel; especially my eldest daughter, Florence, for teaching me some of the ethics in writing. I love you all.

I also thank my pastor, Chris Oyakhilome, whose teachings have moulded my life and exposed me to the truth. 'I have been greatly influenced by you, sir.'

And to many Christian writers whose work had helped me finish this book.

Dedication

I am dedicating this book to the Holy Spirit, the earnest of my salvation, my teacher, my counsellor, my inspiration who inspired me, and gave me the ability and grace to write this book.

To my mother who has gone to be with the Lord, whose life was an example of what marriage should be. She went through thick and thin in her marriage but never gave up till her end.

And to my dad whom I call a noble man—A man who loves God and succeeded in passing on Christianity from his own parents to us, his children, and grandchildren.

Preface

I was motivated by the Word of God through the Holy Spirit to write this book. Many Christian marriages have failed over time due to the lack of understanding of purpose. There is so much confusion in the world today in the search of true purpose. The Holy Spirit has given me a voice to speak out the mind of God concerning the purpose of marriage. I have also taught seminars on marriage to many Christians. The lack of proper understanding and right application of God's Word is the cause of this dilemma. Many see the subject of marriage as a complex subject. God said, 'my people are destroyed for the lack of knowledge'. (Hosea 4: 6). We are all aware that many people, even prominent Christian leaders struggle with the very concept of marriage and divorce. This is because the church has not lifted its head above the natural to critically look into the spiritual meaning and purpose of marriage. Many have endeavoured to tackle this issue, but they have not been very successful because they have not actually found the root cause of the problems.

Many Christians bring in culture into Christianity. Culture and Christianity cannot work together. As a matter of fact, culture is what God has called us out from. He told our father Abraham to leave his land of nativity and go to a new land that he would show him. In other words, God was saying, 'Leave your culture, your beliefs, your lifestyle, come let me introduce you to myself; for my ways are different from your ways'. In God there is no American style or Asian or African style marriage. There is only one style, and it is the Christ-like style. The only way for marriages to work is if we rid ourselves of tradition and cleave to God's Word.

God's purpose for marriage is not for us to be waned down by heartaches and bad experiences, he actually wants us to enjoy the union and celebrate our uniqueness while fulfilling his calling in our lives. This is the place where all of God's children are called to live. Through the leading of the Holy Spirit, I have exposed the mind of God concerning marriage based on the Bible.

Some of the experiences and thoughts of some dear sisters and brothers in the Lord are also discussed in this book. All the chapters of this book are birthed by the Spirit of God, without him I can do nothing. If you are reading this book, according to the grace that is in his Word, it will transform your marriage, taking it to a more fulfilling place in God. A new light will shine; the light of God's Word, the light that will swallow up every form of darkness in your marriage, and bring you into a place of love and peace and joy.

In the years that lie ahead, we are going to experience a dynamic explosion in the body of Christ as a result of truth embraced. I am convinced that marriage will play a crucial role in bringing the body of Christ to the full unity and full stature of Christ.

This book is beneficial to every Christian. It doesn't matter what stage in life you're at. If you are single and hoping to get married someday, it will give you an understanding of what the purpose of marriage is before you get in. If you are already married, it shows you how to live and love the God way. If you are already divorced, it will give you hope.

Chapter One

What Is Marriage?

Modern society and science are trying to give the world a different definition to marriage, which has brought about a misconception of the subject matter. Same sex marriages, which were seen as absurd and frowned at in the past, has now been accepted by the world, even some so-called Christians in the church. Some Anglican parishes made headlines in 2008 when priests were marrying themselves. Jonathan Wynn and Martin Beckford wrote an article they posted on the Internet on the 6 August 2008 that the Archbishop of Canterbury has claimed that 'active homosexual relationships are comparable to marriage in the eyes of God'. Some believe that God actually created some individuals to be homosexuals.

People are moving from place to place confused, miserable, and helpless in search for answers to their questions in regards to marriage. There is chaos everywhere; marriage counsellors are seeing more people than ever before. Marriage seminars are being held all year round. The answer to all this is revealed in the Word of God. The times we live in are dangerous times; the Bible describes it as perilous times, so we must know God's Word for ourselves so that we will not be deceived. Let the Word of God dwell in you richly. People are interpreting the Bible to suit themselves. God's standards can never change even if people try to change it. The world opposes everything that is of God and from God. You must understand that God's will for marriage is based on his Word, so the more of the Scripture you know and understand, the more difficult it will be to get deceived. If you are a Christian, then the Word of God must be the final authority in your life, irrespective of what the world is saying. We live by his Word, and we are also sustained by his Word. Bible says he sustains or upholds all things by the Word of his power. The world's opinion concerning marriage cannot work for a Christian because as my pastor, Chris Oyakhilome, would say, 'We play by a different set of rules'. We belong to a kingdom, and we live by the rules of the kingdom. Our kingdom is superior to this world. The world has nothing to offer, all it has is unhappiness, pain, and gross confusion. But we must understand that our light has come. Christ is the light of the church and of the world.

Marriage Defined

Marriage is a union between a man and a woman kneaded together by love. It is a covenant relationship that joins together the souls of a man and a woman. Marriage is a place for sharing, a place for giving, a place for appreciation, and a place to express faith in one another; it is a place for love, a selfless place, a beautiful place.

It has its origin with God in Garden of Eden where God arranged the first one. Genesis 1: 27-28:

> *'So God created man in his own image, in the image of God created he him; male and female created he them. And God blessed them, and God said unto them, be fruitful and multiply . . .'*

Chapter 2: 24 says, '***Therefore shall a man leave his father and his mother, and shall cleave unto his wife: and they shall be one flesh.***'

Marriage according to God's design is between a man and a woman, not between a man and a man or a woman and a woman. God is the creator of all flesh, and everything that he created was good. He never designed a man for a man; this is one of the many interpretations of medical science. The Bible tells us that Sodom and Gomorra were destroyed because of this very sin. If he once destroyed a nation because of this sin why will he now accept it as normal practice in this generation? Is God unjust? Not a chance. He is indeed a righteous God, and he cannot deny himself. God has never changed; he is the same yesterday, today, and forever. His ordinances are also the same.

Marriage should be between two people who share the same values and believes. If a man marries a woman whose values and beliefs are contrary to his, there will be serious problems in that home; it's like putting two enemy nations under one umbrella. The Bible says in Amos 3: 3:

'Can two walk together except they be agreed?'

Nothing goes well in a home where there is always disagreement. A house that is divided against itself cannot stand. They may have a difference in opinion but not when it comes to the Word of God or the things of God. Marriage is supposed to be enjoyable and not miserable. Marriage between a pagan and a Christian will always struggle to keep its head above the water because they won't agree on the core principles of Christianity. A Christian that marries a non-Christian has deliberately violated God's Word that says a believer should not be unequally yoked with an unbeliever, what has light got with darkness?

Psalm 1: 1 amp says, *'Blessed (happy, fortunate, prosperous and enviable) is the man who walks and lives not in the counsel of the ungodly (following their advise, their plans and purposes) nor stands (submissive and inactive) in the path where sinners walk, nor sits down (to relax and rest) where the scornful (and the mockers) gather. Vs 3 say . . . 'And whatsoever he does shall prosper.'*

It means that those who are uncompromisingly righteous shall prosper. A good friend once asked me an interesting question. She said, 'Mary, how do I know God's choice of man for me because the one I have now doesn't seem to be?' The greatest gift that God gave to mankind apart from his son Jesus is freewill. God gave us the right to choose. If it were not so, God would have stopped Eve from being deceived. Moses said, 'I bring before you life and death, choose life that ye may live'. The truth is always placed before us, but the decision to do right lies within us. God does not force you to marry Peter or John, although he knows who you will choose to marry even before the marriage; He only advices you to marry a true believer for your own good. There was a time when people walk up to ladies and tell them God said you are my wife. Even though the lady does not love that brother in that way, she marries him at the detriment of her happiness because she does not want to disobey God. This is so contrary to his character. He loves you and desires to see you happy, so don't be deceived. All he wants is for you to make right choices.

Prosperity is sure for the one who does not mingle with an unbeliever. This does not mean that we shouldn't talk to them; our ministry to the unbeliever is to win them to Christ.

Most Christians who go into this kind of marriages, go in, sincerely thinking they'll change the other into the kind of person they would like them to be. Wrong move! Only God's Word has the capacity to change a person because the Word of God is living and active, sharper than any double-edged sword. It penetrates even to dividing soul and spirit, joints and marrow; it judges the thoughts and attitudes of the heart. Jesus said, 'the words that I speak unto you, they are spirit and they are life' (John 6: 63). Don't trust yourself to change your spouse rather trust in God's Word to do it.

Now if you are in this situation, your spouse is not yet saved, start now to pray for the salvation of your spouse. As you pray, you must be an example of light. You are the light that your spouse sees; you represent Christ. If you behave contrary to what you preach, how can your spouse change? What will attract them to your Christ? Therefore, let your conduct be worthy of the Gospel. Be diligent in praying and watch God transform your spouse.

A lady from a Christian background fell in love with a Muslim; she loved him so much that she agreed to marry him immediately he proposed. She ignored the warnings of her family and friends and went ahead and married him. 'He allows me go to church because he believes there's only one God,' she would defend. Just few months after the marriage, he stopped her from going to church and forced her to denounce her faith. Life without Christ for this woman is torture. She follows him to where he serves his own god, but deep down in her heart she prays to the almighty, no longer free to openly declare Christ. She lives in a spiritual prison as a result of her mistake. God can never deceive us, his Word is truth. How can we understand God's purpose of instituting marriage if we compromise?

We can't afford to take our salvation for granted, for it was purchased with too high a price. It cost God his son, Jesus, the wonder of heaven, to reconcile us back to himself. No wonder, the Bible says to work out your salvation with fear and trembling. There is absolutely no reason for a Christian to compromise with the devil; Bible says he has come to kill, to steal, and to destroy. He will destroy your life if you let him, because he opposes everything that is of God. John 4: 4 says, 'ye are of God little children . . .'

What Is Living Together?

Living together is a mutual informal agreement between a man and a woman to live together and participate in everything that constitutes a marriage without being legally joined together by a court or a church. Some unsaved folks who are afraid of commitment would prefer that. A woman once told me that marriage is the reason why people take so much from each other in divorce courts, 'if they're not legally married, they won't have to share their assets,' she said. Can you see how selfish that is? It may sound all right with the world, but it is not acceptable for a child of God; living together with someone that you're not married to will short circuit the power of the Holy Spirit in your lives, his manifestations will not be evident in your lives because you're living in sin. It is called fornication, a breeding ground for demons. Anyone could put up an argument that Adam and Eve did not have a formal marriage ceremony, true! But I'm not talking about a ceremony; a couple could get married quietly without all that expensive parties; it's about the authority that joins them together as man and wife. The Bible says that God caused a deep sleep and took out a rib from Adam, and made Eve. When Adam woke up, God presented Eve to him and blessed them, commanding them to increase, multiply, and to subdue the earth. So we see that God joined them together and blessed them. Jesus confirmed it by saying, 'What God has joint together, let not man put asunder'.

A marriage must be officiated by a higher authority to make it legal. It could be a church pastor or a court, with a group of witnesses. Christians marry in the church, and as the officiating pastor pronounces them as husband and wife, the name of the Lord seals them together. A man cannot wake up one day, ring up his girlfriend and say, 'From today henceforth you are my wife and I am your husband'. Something has to happen as a proof that she is his wife. That proof is marriage officiated by a higher authority. God was the highest authority that officiated Adam's marriage to Eve. He was their covering, before their fall they didn't know they were naked. He will be for you a covering and a shield today if you let him, for he has not changed. He was a covering for the children of Israel in the wilderness. The Bible records that he manifested himself as a cloud in the day, and at night a flame of fire. When God is the covering in your marriage, it means that when the enemy throws his fiery darts, they will not touch you. It also means that when trials and temptations come, he will make a way of escape for you. The Word of God says that when the enemy comes, like a flood the Lord will lift up a standard against him.

I have seen Christians living together unmarried, and if that is you, I want you to know that it is biblically wrong; honour God with your bodies, do the right thing and be happy. Pray for the Spirit of God to minister to both of you so that you can go ahead and do the right thing.

God loves us so much; He gives us an example to live by, for our own good. I would like to encourage you that are about getting married to be sure that your foundation is not faulty because if you build on a bad foundation, you will not find purpose and, some day, your house will surely fall; it will not stand the test of time. Build your marriage on Christ, our solid foundation, our rock and our shield. When the wind of life blows your way, you will be unshakeable because you built on a solid foundation. Make the Word of God the platform on which you make your decisions, and let it be your benchmark. A dear sister once told me her experiences during courtship. She was dating a so-called Christian brother who had proposed marriage to her. She had always been attending weekly prayer meeting in church even before she met him. One day, he came looking for her only to be told that she had gone to church again, so he decided to wait. On her arrival, he got angry and complained about her frequency in the church. The dear sister walked away and pondered about what had happened. She thought if he could begin from then to complain about her church attendance, he could stop her from going to church once they got married, so she decided to call of the engagement. He was a wolf in sheep's clothing. A couple of years later, she got married to a pastor. God honoured her because she did not compromise her faith.

Courtship

Courtship is helpful and very much encouraged, but you cannot know everything about a person you don't live with, and there are certain things that will only be exposed when you actually start living together as married couples. But courtship is the opportunity you've got to actually know those things about your supposed spouse that you would have found out after marriage. I have seen many newly-weds accusing one another for being pretentious during courtship; it is a common occurrence. Sometimes the excitement of getting married blindfolds people; they may not be very observant about the behaviour patterns of the one they are about to marry. One could be pretentious, but he or she will occasionally sell themselves out. True self will be exposed when real crisis occur. At such times, the individual is off guard and so their reactions to these crises will be seen. Sex during courtship beclouds your judgement of the one you are about to marry. Bible teaches abstinence, but abstinence is not denial. If you truly want to know more about your spouse, then consciously observe how they react when faced with all kinds of situation, for example, money. Money is one of the causes of divorce, so it will be wise to understand what your fiancé's opinion is about it. You need the wisdom of God to be able to discern rightly. Without the help of the Spirit of God, you will be misled. In the book of Daniel, the Holy Spirit is described as 'the revealer of secrets'.

He will reveal everything that you need to know about the person you intend to marry.

Most people go into marriage with very high expectations, hoping for the other to keep them happy. It is essential for us to know that true happiness comes from above.

Furthermore, the Bible tells that the joy of knowing the Lord is our strength. (Emphasis added.) As Christians, our joy and happiness flows from within us, even our spirits. When I and Chris first got married, I knew he was everything I ever wanted; he dressed the way I like, and he made jokes the way I like, his passion for sweet cars did not help matters also, all that apart, he loves the Lord. I fell head over heels in love with him. About a couple of years after, I realised that there was more to him than I knew about, even though we had proper counselling sessions that did impart our lives, but I had to learn during those tough years about what true love is. It's not about right or wrong, it's unconditional. It is giving out love and expecting nothing back. We became students of the Holy Spirit as he gradually thought us how to look beyond faults and love unconditionally.

Prayer

Dear heavenly father, you are the joy of the whole earth. Thank you for the gift of marriage. Your plans and thoughts for me are for good. Help me lord to do away with any relationship that will hinder my communion with the Holy Spirit. I will glorify you in my body knowing that my body is your dwelling place. As I go on living this good life that you gave me, may your glory be seen in me by all. I pray this in Jesus name. Amen

Chapter Two

A Selfless Love

If we were to define what love is, we would say so many beautiful and inspiring things, like love is the strongest adhesive that binds hearts together, and some would liken it to a strong feeling of affection linked with sexual attraction and so on. Christ is that strong adhesive that synchronises hearts together. He is the necessary ingredient that makes marriage work. Since we live by God's Word, let's go to the Bible to see what it says about love and its origin. 1 John 4: 7-8 says:

> *'Beloved, let us love one another: for love is of God; and everyone that loveth is born of God, and knoweth God. He that loveth not knoweth not God; for God is love.'*

Love Originates from God and We are Born of His Love

Love springs from God, and it originates from him, so we as children of God must walk in God's love, for therein we are born. If you are a born-again Christian, you are born of love. If we are identified with God, then we should be identified with his kind of love also. The Spirit of God has thought me that whether we be in a marriage relationship or not, we are all one in Christ, and we have one father (John 20: 17). Marriage is spiritual; it is a divine relationship, so we cannot operate it with a human love. Human or natural love is too weak to operate in this great union. It endures but for a while; it's very fleshy and touchy. The God kind of love is deep down in the spirit; it is peaceful, it is simple, and it is quiet. It endures hardships and is willing to suffer wrong. Marriage is a place where we express God's love to one another in truth.

Marriage will become sacred to you when you see past the natural and see from the realm of the spirit; a deeper understanding suddenly comes to you and you become conscious of the glorious life to which we've been called to live, both now and hereafter. Learn to see your spouse from the eyes of Jesus, those eyes of mercy and love.

The quality of life we live is a direct result of what influences us; a person who is intoxicated by alcohol is subject to its influence and as a result will produce according to the dictates of the alcohol. Likewise, if you are influenced by God's love, you will produce the fruits of love. The Bible says that the love of God is shared abroad in your heart so much so that agape (unconditional love) becomes expressed in our lives and in our relationship with our spouses.

Marriage Is Only for This Earth Realm

You are first Christians, before anything else. Your spouses are first to you—fellow partakers of the body of Christ—before being a husband or a wife because that which is spiritual is before the physical. John 20: 17 shows that we all have one father and one God. Marriage is only for this earth realm; in heaven there is no marriage. We are all together called the 'bride of Christ'. For the lesser shall be swallowed up by the greater. Isn't it amazing that the Bible did not distinguish between male and female, and the moment we step into eternity we become the same. Therefore, let us enjoy the time that we spent together as husband and wife because we can never get this time back. Your spouse is more than a partner; he or she is one of whom Christ, the son of the most high God, died. God has placed a very high value on our lives; we know this because of the value of the price he paid to save us. We ought also to cherish and value one another in like manner.

Jesus said in Mathew 11: 29:

> *'Take my yoke upon you and learn of me; for I am meek and lowly in heart: and you shall find rest unto your souls.'*

Jesus is our example; he is the husband of the church, and he has shown us an example of true love, for we were still in our sins when he died for us. His death was not conditioned on our rightness rather on God's righteousness, and his love looks beyond our faults. Jesus knew that Peter would deny him three times in his greatest hour of anguish; he knew that Judas would betray him; he also knew that Thomas would doubt his resurrection; he knew that the people of Israel would choose Barabbas, a thief in his stead after all the miracles he performed in their midst; he knew that you and I will fail him from time to time, yet he went to the cross for us. Jesus's love looks for solution rather than giving up; he bought the whole world with his love. Today we are all beneficiaries of his love. The Word of God will work for anybody who dares to put it to work. You that is going through terrible situations in your marriage, I want you to know that God does not take pleasure in seeing you afflicted; he has made you more than a conqueror, therefore match the grace of God versus that situation that you're facing and you will find out that, that challenge that seems like a giant is actually bread for you. Take advantage of the grace that is in Christ Jesus; it will carry you over. The Word of God is guaranteed.

See to it that love reigns in your home because where the love of God is; there also you'll find God's peace. He calls it shalom in Hebrew, which translates peace. It means peace heaped upon peace on every side. Peace in your marriage, in your finances, among your children, all around peace. We must thrive to love as God loves; love will take away all the heartaches. This grace to see marriage in this light was granted me by the Holy Spirit; he said when you have sought him with all your heart, you will find him. He opened my eyes to see what the cure is for the marital problems the church is facing in these last days. I call it the end time distractions. The cure is an unconditional love.

Some people might think that God's standard of love is too high to attain, but not to worry if you are a spirit-filled believer, for you've already got it. According to Galatians 5: 22, you have it in you.

> *'But the fruit of the spirit is love, joy, peace, long suffering, gentleness, goodness, faith, meekness, temperance . . .'*

So you see, love is one of the fruits of the spirit. When the Holy Spirit indwells you, love will be manifested in your life, just be conscious of it and decide to work it out. My pastor always says there is no body in this world that he cannot love; he may not like their attitude but he sure loves them. For some time I wondered how possible that is, I understood later that the reason is because he sees them through the eyes of Jesus—an unconditional love.

Your Spouse Is a Gift from God, Treat Them As Such

During those years when my marriage was going through turbulence, the Holy Spirit asked me to imagine if something had just fallen from heaven and if I knew it was a gift from God for me, how would I treat it. And I thought I would cherish it all my life, I would let everybody know I got a gift from God, and I would be extremely honoured by God to have sent something all the way from heaven to me. And then he said, 'Your husband is that gift from God, treat him as you have said'. From that day, my attitude changed for better. I began to see him as a God-given gift. I decided to show him love in spite of how I feel, and the Spirit of God sensitised him also to respond to the love that I was giving him; as a result, we became more tolerable to each other, and we found true happiness. We saw evidence that the wisdom of God is better than choice gold. I want you to know that your spouse is a gift from God, treat him or her accordingly.

There are some spouses who are always very kind to people they meet outside, but when they get home, they are completely unapproachable. It is hard to have a simple conversation with them without an argument. They love to be seen as a dear brother or sister, but when they get home it's a different ball game. They may be happy out there with friends or fellow believers, but as soon as they get home, their countenance changes, and they make everyone else uncomfortable. If you behave in this manner, you will only succeed in hindering God's blessings from flowing in your life.

Every Man Has a King in Him

Find out the strengths of your spouse and learn to build on them, capitalise on them, and before long you'll see they're better at what they do best. Acknowledge every virtue and encourage them; it's like planting a seed and watering it to grow. Help your spouse to see prospects in that which they know how to do. As you encourage them, you will attract admiration and respect to yourself. The Bible says in Proverbs 11: 25 that 'he that watereth shall himself be watered'. On the other hand, you must learn also to kill each other's weaknesses. I know you're already asking how? The way to kill your weakness is by not feeding it. If you do not feed a plant, it will not grow. Each time you complain about their mistakes, you've just fed that weakness, and each time you get bitter and resentful, it's just had a good meal and so it will grow and produce more of such behaviours because that person will naturally want to defend himself; the arguments becomes unending and eventually your home will become a living hell. Naturally speaking, every man has a king in him; if you approach the king in him, you are sure to get what you want, but if you approach him foolishly, he will show you foolishness. In a kingdom, a king that receives praise, honour, and respect from his people will satisfy them with plenty, but a king whose people dishonour and disrespect him will be very cruel to them. You must be wise in your dealing with one another; do not take each other for granted and live peaceably with one another.

Prayer

Dear heavenly father, you are the epitome of love. I thank you for the opportunity i have to hear your word. Thank you for giving me the gift of a spouse. You demonstrated your love for me on the cross where your son died unconditionally for me. Help me to love selflessly the way you do. May my love for my spouse grow day by day, and as I yield myself to you may your love flood my heart and fill my environment in Jesus name. Amen.

Chapter Three

The Purpose of Marriage

People marry for various reasons—some for love, some because of their cultural orientation, and others to have children. For those that marry because of having children, I want to ask, what if after marriage you find out that your wife is unable to have children or your husband is impotent. Then is your purpose for getting married not defeated? Some marry because their biological clock is ticking; this is a term that the world has coined to say that they are getting old. Some marry because of societal pressures and so on. I have heard of a man who said he wants to get married so that he will have tax relief from the government. It sounds unbelievable, but he truly believes that if he gets married, he will save more by paying less tax.

The primary purpose is not to have children because the Bible says that children are a reward from God; they are the fruit that comes as a result of marriage. The purpose of marriage is not to meet up with the expectation of family and friends because when problems arise, they will only give a word of advice and you will be left alone to fix it. And if you fail, they will also be the first to tag you as a divorcee. It is wrong to do anything because people want you to, do things because God wants you to do it. If you live according to his will, all of heaven backs you up and you are sure to have the victory.

It is of utmost necessity that we understand clearly the reason for marriage. Most people have also misplaced the purpose with the roles. The purpose is different from the roles. We shall discuss the roles in detail in subsequent chapters, and by God's grace we'll all understand the difference. The Bible says that the entrance of his Words gives light, it gives understanding, and it illuminates darkness and helps us see the truth.

Truth Brings Wholeness to Your Marriage

Beloved brethren, the understanding of what I am about to explain to you through the Holy Spirit will bring wholeness back to your marriage if only you will pay attention to it. As you read on, if your mind sways away from the book, be conscious and bring your mind back by subjecting it to the Word of God because these are the revelations of the Spirit of God for the church. He has exposed the mind of God-concerning marriage.

Now let's go to the Word to find what God's purpose is. Genesis 2:18 says:

> *'And the Lord God said, it is not good that the man should be alone; I will make him an help suitable for him.'*

Mark the word 'alone' and 'help'. I want you to understand that woman was not God's original idea. According to Genesis 2: 2-3, he had ended his work and rested on the seventh day he had already sanctified and blessed his day of rest. The Bible records that all he created was good even without Eve. So at what point then did Eve come on the scene. It was when God saw the loneliness of Adam in verse 18. Every animal was made after their kind, male and female.

Adam was the only one without a companion. When God saw that, he said it is not good for Adam to be alone. At that point, God created Eve from Adam and then presented her to him as his wife. Be careful to notice that Adam named his wife as he named the animals; he named her woman because she was his kind taken out of him. He called her flesh of my flesh and bone of my bone. As a man do you consider and treat your wife as flesh of your flesh or do you treat her as a separate being? I find it fascinating that God did not explain to Adam how Eve was created; Adam knew by revelation. So you see, if Eve had not eaten of the fruit of the knowledge of good and evil, she would have still known all things through revelation. Woman is taken out of man and man is born of woman; we are all one, no wonder God said the two shall be one flesh.

The union of Adam and Eve was for companionship. Adam was not lonely because he had all the animals around him, and every now and then God comes down to talk with him in the garden. But the Bible says that he was alone, meaning, he was one of his kind. There was no other like Adam. All the other animals had their kind. So when God saw it, it displeased him and he said it is not good for the man to be alone. Being alone is not fun at all; nobody truly loves to be alone. How boring life would be without someone to share it with. If you ever find someone that loves to be alone in this world, be sure that that fellow has a big problem; his or her mind has become a playground for the enemy. Make haste to begin interceding in prayers for such a one. Everyone loves to feel loved, and everyone loves to be celebrated. It is a human need. It was also good for Adam to have someone of his kind that he would love and in return be loved by the same one. Notice I said 'by the same one'. Most married people have cultivated a bad and sinful habit of keeping concubines. You cannot get happier by keeping more than one woman or man. A certain man once said he was keeping a second woman as a standby generator so that if one fails the other will kick off. How sinful and fleshy that is. Such thoughts and desires come from the enemy only for the eventual destruction of those that yield themselves to such.

Now going back to our text in Genesis, remember that God had given to Adam the responsibility of replenishing and cultivating the garden before Eve came on the scene. That was Adam's assignment. Now when God saw that Adam was alone, he said 'I will make him a ***help*** suitable for him'. It means therefore that Adam, not only that he was alone, but also had to carry out his God-given task, which is the above mentioned, of which he would need help. Isn't it typical of the great commission that our master, Jesus the Christ, has given to all who believe in him, to preach the Gospel to every creature? We cannot be effective with our God-given assignment if we do not have the help and support of one another.

So as revealed by the Word of God, the purpose of marriage is for companionship, friendship and intimacy.To help each other in fulfilling God's purpose for our lives and to create a family unit where godly men and women will be raised because God seeks a godly offspring from this union called marriage. Praise God.

God had planned our lives before we ever showed up in this world. Before we were conceived in our mother's womb, he knew us. He knew what day we would be born and what name that we would be called. He knew whether we would accept him as our Saviour or reject the sacrifice of his dear son. He knows what part each of us will play in the ministry of reconciliation. He knows our end from our beginning. Ephesians 1: 4-5 proves that we have been predestined. It reads:

> *'According as he hath chosen us in him before the foundation of the world, that we should be holy and without blame before him in love: having predestinated us unto the adoption of children by Jesus Christ to himself, according to the good pleasure of his will . . .'*

And also Ephesians 2: 10 from the amplified version says:

> *'For we are God's own handiwork (his workmanship), recreated in Christ Jesus, (born anew) that we may do those good works which God predestined (planned before hand) for us (taking paths which he prepared ahead of time), that we should walk in them (living the good life which he prearranged and made ready for us to live).'*

From these Scriptures we know that God has predestined us for good works, and there are some that God had called into ministry for the purpose of building up the church. Some, God hath called into the business world for the purpose of financing the Gospel. If you are a pastor, God had given you your spouse as a suitable help to accompany you and to help you fulfil his purpose, just as Adam was given a suitable help. If you are a business person, your spouse had been given as a help. Some people put their spouses out of their plans when it comes to their businesses and careers. Their partners are completely put in the dark. If you are one of those and you're successful all by yourself, imagine if both of you are working together, how great will that success be. The Bible says that one will chase a thousand but two will chase ten thousand. You're better off working together, and that is the perfect will of God.

Don't Ignore or Neglect Your Help

Success is not achieved single-handed; apart from the Holy Spirit who is our ultimate help, there is someone who physically stands by and supports you, accompanies you, and encourages you, and most of the time that person is your spouse. Your spouse is a grace from God. Do not receive the grace of God in vain; take advantage of God's grace in your life. God gives you help so that you will succeed and prosper in your endeavours.

In any field you are, your overall success benefits the body of Christ in general. If you are a business person, you must understand that the reason he gives you help is to make you prosper so that you will financially support global evangelism. Deuteronomy 8: 18 shows us the purpose for prosperity.

> *'But thou shall remember the lord thy God: for it is he that giveth thee power to get wealth that he may establish his covenant which he sware unto thy fathers as it is this day.'*

Jesus came to seek and save that which was lost, and we are partners with him in doing that. He did it with his own life, and so we must do it with our money, our time, and effort. If it comes to dying for the Gospel, we should be ready. So many Christians around the world have been martyred for the sake of the Gospel that we freely enjoy.

Just as God gave Adam the responsibility of replenishing the earth and caring for the garden, so also Jesus has given us the responsibility of seeking and saving the lost. And he has given us each other as help to carry out his divine purpose. The purpose of marriage is to help one another to do the will of God.

There are so many notable couples today in ministry whose lives are worthy of emulation. They are at the forefront of world evangelism, producing results significantly for the kingdom of God. The reason for their success is because they are twain, yielded to one another and to the Holy Spirit, ministering to the needs of one another while carrying out God's purpose for their lives. These ministers are used by God to prepare the generation next for the work of the ministry. May God richly bless those that work in his vineyard, spreading the Gospel around the world, giving hope to a dying world using their time and money; may God reward their labour of love. They are indeed worthy of emulation. Philippians 4: 8 commends us to think, meditate, and copy things that are true, pure, and noble of good report, of virtue, and of praise.

If we work together as husband and wife, we are sure to get the best results in our God-given tasks, and this applies to every discipline in life, not only in ministry.

A dear man of God was sharing his testimony in church. He said he always got nervous standing on the pulpit; he was having some difficulty in preaching, so he got home and expressed his concern to his wife. She looked at him and said, 'Honey, you are a good preacher everybody knows that, and even the demons in hell know that'. On hearing those words he was encouraged to go ahead and fulfil God's call for his life. The union of marriage is so beautiful; we can be a source of encouragement to one another, especially when we face challenges. The words of this dear woman of God gave her pastor husband the confidence he needed to carry on his God-given assignment.

The Great Commission

We all have been given a great commission, so we cannot be distracted. Dr Frederick Price once said if you are the only one that God has on earth, is God in trouble? Oh, if we would only understand God's purpose for marriage, it will take us out of those marital problems that so easily distract us. Then we can forge a mighty army for Jesus. Bible says in Deuteronomy 32: 30 that one shall chase a thousand, two shall put ten thousand to flight, but we are more than two, three, four, and five, so come on, let's take the world for Jesus.

God depends on us to win souls to the kingdom, and we cannot let him down. We know that it is not God's will that any should perish but that all should come to repentance. This ought to be our focus, the will of the father, and nothing else. The world should see the love of God in our eyes, in our words, and in our actions. That's how they'll know that truly God is love. Our Lord, Jesus, before he went into glory, said his followers should feed the hungry, clothe the naked, visit the sick and those that are in prison, alongside preaching the Gospel. As we act in obedience to his commands, we get blessed, and the world will also recognise us as the sons of God. Let us not rub the world of their opportunity to see God's glory manifested through our marriages. Remember, he comes with his reward in his hand, will he find us diligent to our heavenly call or will he find us in marital problems?

Prayer

Lord, you are the monarch of the universe. I have clearly understood your reason for instituting this great union called marriage. May your purpose for marriage be fulfilled in mine. As I unreservedly give myself to your word, may your glory and your presence fill my family and transform the life of my family members. Thank you for your love and glorious blessings that I experience in my marriage in Jesus name. Amen

Chapter Four

The Distinct Roles in Marriage

There are roles in marriage, God has made it so. The society we live in has redefined the roles, but in the beginning it was not so. God has given us specific roles to play in this union. These roles do not imply that the man is more superior to the woman nor the woman more superior to the man. As a matter of fact, Galatians 3: 28 tells us that there is neither male nor female because we are all one in Christ. God has given us these roles in the union for organisation purposes. So whether you are the man or the woman, your God-given role is beautiful and it suits you; don't try to be the other, it is not useful; all it can help to do is to facilitate problems. God has given to us skills and abilities to help us function effectively in our individual roles; it means, therefore, that all we need to function effectively is in the inside of us. When you are functioning in your role it feels natural, instinctively you just know what to do about a given task and also how to do it.

Displacement of Roles Is the Birth of Conflicts

The man cannot take the place of the woman; he will not be effective because he hasn't gotten the grace for it. A man who decides not to work but stay home to do domestic chores will feel very frustrated after day two, but the woman will do it with ease. Likewise, the woman should not assume her husband's role. If a woman takes on the role of feeding the family and paying for house rent for any reason, whether he lost his job or his take home pay is insufficient, the man after a while may begin to feel incompetent in the home; they love to be in charge because by assignment God has put them in charge. Some men's reaction may be to have extramarital relationships outside the home where they could be in charge. I have heard women complaining about how hard they work to keep the family going but that their husbands have been caught cheating. The reason is that they feel out of place even if their wife's intention was good. Some might resort to drinking just because they are unable to perform in their role as the head. God has made the man the leader or the head of the home and his role as a leader is his pride or his ego, so when you take that away from him, he has nothing left. Aside, assuming his role will keep the woman frazzled, confused, and frustrated because she was not designed for that. There is a more excellent way for the woman to assist in financial issues. Let's take this as an example, a woman who wants to support her husband with the house rent, rather than giving him the money to settle the landlord, she goes to the landlord herself while her husband is home doing nothing. That man is sure to feel embarrassed even though his wife was trying to help. If that continues, he may not say a word about that but he may find consolation elsewhere.

The distinction of roles in marriage has brought about several topics of debate in the body of Christ. These issues have been dealt with in the Bible, and there is no mincing of words. Some claim that the cause of divorce is as a result of misinterpretations of the word in regards to the issue of wives' submission to their husbands. Those who claim that their marriages broke because of the traditional teaching of submission are not actually true to themselves; it is their refusal to submit to their husband's leadership that actually caused the divorce. Remember, there is a way that seems right to a man but the end is destruction. The divorce rate in this generation is higher than in older generation. So the teaching is not the problem; it is the individual's unwillingness to adhere that causes the problem. The Word of God cannot cause us to stumble. God is faithful. The law itself is good, so declares the Bible, but the people could not keep it. So sin took advantage of the opportunity and produced all kinds of sinful desires. Now God, through Christ Jesus, has redeemed us from the law and brought us under grace, and this grace helps us become doers of the Word and not people trying to obey.

The law says 'thou shall not commit adultery'. Do we now commit adultery because we are now under grace? Not so. The law came like a schoolmaster guiding us to the path of righteousness. The submission of wife to her husband's leadership did not come through the law but under the dispensation of grace.

Now bringing that into marriage, Ephesians 5: 22-23 admonishes women to submit to their own husbands, but before that the preceding verse says, submit to one another. It actually means we all as the body of Christ in general should submit to one another, and in the verse 23, the Apostle Paul brought it down to the family unit. He specifically addressed wives. A woman's submission to her husband is in his leadership, while a man's responsibility to his wife is in his service.

We Are Born of an Incorruptible Seed

The challenges we all face in our marriages are the test of our faith and obedience to the Word. The Bible never said all will be easy, but it sure says that the Holy Spirit bears us up in our weaknesses. When the Spirit of God is at work in your life, he empowers you and gives you the ability to do all things. The reason for divorce is because our love is not perfect; our love is not an unconditional love. God has not called us to live an impossible Christian life. He has equipped us and graced us to live a triumphant and victorious Christian life in Christ. There is an attack in marriages in the body of Christ, and the purpose of this attack is to make the church unstable and weak. If the devil attacks marriages, he has attacked the family system causing disorientation in our children. That is his plan. But thanks to God, we are born of an incorruptible seed of God's Word.

Why are we blaming ourselves for the high rate of divorce and the devil that is the mastermind behind it is left alone? We are the body of Christ, a victorious church, members of the general assembly in heaven. We must come together in unity, with one voice and rebuke the devil out of our homes, out of our marriages and out of our churches. Our weapons of war are not carnal, but they are mighty through God to the pulling down of strong holds. Divorce is a strong hold that must be taken down.

Prayer

Dear lord, you are the great and awesome God. You have ordained me to live a life of victory, progress and success everyday, and I rejoice in that knowledge. Thank you for giving me the skills and ability I need to function effectively in my God—given role in marriage. I declare that through your spirit, I am making progress by studying your word and doing what it says, and your word in me cannot be corrupted, it will surely produce result in Jesus name. Amen

Chapter Five

The Role of a Christian Man

As the Head or Leader

Now, the Scripture says that the man is the head of the woman and the head of man is Christ (1 Cor. 11: 3). He is crowned with God's glory. His leadership according to the Scripture is likened to that of Christ over the church. It should be taken very seriously because he is accountable to Christ as to how he heads the family. The manager of a company is responsible for all the staff in that company and also responsible for the effective running of the company. Now if anything goes wrong, the owner of the company holds the manager responsible, not the employees. As a man you are responsible for your family and you will be held accountable to God as to how you head the home. It's something to be taken seriously. For the man to be an effective leader, he must be uncompromisingly submitted to God. He must first take the spec out of his own eyes so that he can see clearly and remove the plank out of his wife's eye. The Word of God must be the final authority in his own life. The man should understand that the position of a leader is also position to serve. Being a leader is far from being a dictator. A good leader makes his subordinates to want to do a task, not under compulsion but willingly.

He carries everyone on the same page. Jesus washed the feet of his disciples, and it caused them to be unreservedly submissive to his leadership. They were willing to die for the sake of Jesus. Paul was beheaded, Peter was crucified, and the rest of the disciples died following this good leader, Jesus. A woman will unreservedly give herself to a good leader because women crave leadership. Have you ever observed when two lions are fighting over being territorial head? All the cobs and the lionesses stay at bay and watch to see who wins. When the fight is over, they all submit willingly to the strongest lion. The reason is that they feel protected by a strong leader. They are sure of their safety under his leadership. It is one of the characteristics of mammals even women.

To Love His Wife

This kind of love is an unconditional love as I have emphasised in previous chapters. Ephesians 5: 25-28 clearly shows us how. It says:

> *'Husbands, love your wives even as Christ also loved the church and gave himself for it; that he might sanctify and cleanse it with the washing of water by the word, that he might present it to himself a glorious church not having spot, or wrinkle, or any such thing; but that it should be holy and without blemish. So men ought to love their wives as their own bodies. He that loveth his wife loveth himself.'*

Christ's love for us compels us to love each other. Isn't it amazing how Christ's love for the church is compared to a man's love for his wife? A man's love for his wife is sacrificial; he takes responsibility for her mistakes even to the point of death because while we were still in our sins, in our fallen state, Christ died for us (Rom. 3: 23).

If your wife has an attitude, it is an indication of her weakness; she needs to be shown more love and kindness because love conquers all things, even death. No one can resist the power of true love. Wash her constantly with the Word of God. You might not see the changes immediately. Don't despair, keep on loving and caring. With prayers, she will respond eventually because love always wins. Isn't it like Jesus, his love for us took him to the cross, not willing to see us suffer eternal condemnation. But thanks be unto God, his love has brought us back home. The man expresses his love for his wife by appreciating her efforts, and also letting her know what great help she is to him, complimenting her beauty, even if she is overweight she's still beautiful because true beauty is in the character. You don't have to flatter her in trying to give her compliments; there must be something good in her that you can truly appreciate. Love sees good in others. There is one striking thing in the Scripture above; the last sentence of that Scripture is something to think about. It says, 'He that loves his wife loves himself'. In other words, if you don't love your wife, you don't love yourself. It's that simple. Remember, the two shall be one flesh. You do not use a hammer to hit your finger, so why do you hit her? You do not talk bad about yourself, so why would you talk bad of her? Christ commands you to treat her as you would treat yourself. Part of loving her is spending some quality time with her out of your busy schedules.

Live with Your Wife According to Knowledge

Magnify your position as the head, not dominating her but dealing with her with wisdom, knowing that she is the weaker vessel in respect to her physical orientation. Just as a doctor knows medicine and a lawyer knows the law, a man ought to know his wife. Know her strengths and her weaknesses. When you learn her and understand her, you will find it much easier to lead her. In some cultures, the man sees the woman as working robot. You see a couple coming back from shopping, with the woman carrying all the groceries walking behind, while the man takes the lead walking ahead empty-handed. She is supposed to be your help. You will also find in some homes where the woman is busy cooking and at the same time taking care of the children, and the man sitting down in the couch reading the morning papers, not willing to help. It is wiser to give a hand any time your assistance is needed and not to be rigid as in division of labour.

1 Peter 3: 7 says:

> *'Likewise, ye husbands, dwell with them according to knowledge, giving honour unto the wife as unto the weaker vessel, and as being heirs together of the grace of life; that your prayers be not hindered.'*

Now this is getting very interesting. The answers to your prayers are depended on how you treat your wife. You can't afford to have your prayers hindered; all your plans, hopes, and ambitions are on the line. If you lack wisdom in this area, ask of the father who liberally gives to all who ask so that you will deal wisely.

As a Decision-Maker

The decisions that one take in life has a long-term effect on that individual, whether negative or positive. The right decisions you make will cause an increase in your family. It could be an increase of money, increase of joy and peace, or an increase of success. Therefore it is crucial to make right decisions. The wisdom of God in man will lead him to make right decisions at all times. One of the ministries of the Holy Spirit is to give us good counsel; he is our wonderful counsellor. When a man is yielded to the Spirit of God, he makes good decisions. Now, he can get his wife involved in the process, listening to her own opinion about the issue at hand because the Holy Spirit could also use her to speak to him, but the man has to make the final decision. He does not compromise his stand in Christ even in the face of oppositions, he maintains his stand. A husband should never leave decision making to the wife because she's not designed to be a decision-maker over the man, which makes her vulnerable to mistakes. When God promised Abraham a child, he was in a time of waiting, so Sarah not only advised him but decided that he goes with her maid. It was a wrong counsel because it wasn't God's will. Abraham was supposed to reject that advice and stick with God's promise, but he rather pleased his wife. That was the biggest mistake he ever made because the child of promise according to God's will, will be from Sarah. He finally got separated with the child from that union, Ishmael. Till today the problems in the Middle East originated from Father Abraham's mistake.

Adam made the same mistake. God gave Adam an instruction not to eat of the tree of good and evil. God specifically told him that the day he eats of that tree he shall die. But Eve, after being deceived by the serpent, made a decision for herself and for her husband to disobey God. Bible says that Adam was not deceived. He deliberately allowed Eve to have it her way. And as a result of that, death began to reign till this day. Death is not just the cessation of life, but also a separation from God. Adam was first separated from God and died after hundreds of years. See Romans 5: 17. By now you might be thinking that if Papa Abraham could make that kind of mistake then no man can do it right. Remember that the Holy Spirit had not come then. Right now we are in the dispensation of the Spirit of God; you can do all things through him.

Some women feel that their husbands are not capable of making right decisions, so they try as hard as they can to impress their opinion on the men or to manipulate him so that the man does exactly as they have suggested. It is wrong to do that, allow him to make the decisions. No man truly wants to fail. If a man is left alone to make decisions, him knowing that the success or failure of the family depends on the quality of his decisions, he will be very serious about it. He will involve God every step of the way to help him make the right decision.

He Gives Spiritual Guidance

He teaches his family the Word of God; he brings them before God in prayers daily and instructs them in the way of the Lord. You could do that with a good daily devotional. I love God's testimony about Abraham in Genesis 18: 19. God said:

> *'For I know him, that he will command his children and his household after him, and they shall keep the way of the lord, to do justice and judgement; that the lord may bring upon Abraham that which he hath spoken of him.'*

Dear husband, does God know you as a man like Abraham? Can God boast about your commitment in raising godly children? Pause and think about that. This is God's testimony about Abraham, a man that lived without the indwelling of the Holy Ghost. You are in a better position today because the Spirit of God resides in you permanently, causing you to do right. The Word says when you instruct your household in God's way, the Lord will cause that which he hath spoken concerning you to come to pass. It is beneficial to yield to the Word of God.

The family is a place where godly men and women are raised, so it is important that the man being the leader should lead by example. Children learn more from what they see their parents do. If the man is one that spends time in the Word of God and in prayers, the wife and children also will imbibe that character. It is so important to teach them as they grow up; that all the challenges they will ever face in life has its solution in the Word of God. The Bible says that if they are brought up in this light, they will not depart from it.

I once heard a preacher on TV testifying about God's faithfulness. He said a certain woman was attacked by a man on the road on certain day. The intention of the man was to rape her; she struggled with him as hard as her strength could go but to no avail, and he succeeded. According to the testimony, while the man was on the very act, she suddenly remembered what her grandma had taught her as a child, that if she ever finds herself in trouble to call the name of Jesus. As she shouted the name of Jesus out of desperation three times, the man died on her. It is indeed true that what you teach your children in regards to the Word will never leave them, and it will save them in the day of trouble.

Provision of Food and Shelter

This is where the man's finances come to play. He handles the finances of the family. He is solely responsible to provide for the basic needs of his family. Back in the garden, after the fall, God never told the woman to till the ground to produce food, but he specifically gave that responsibility to Adam. God had given this responsibility to the man. 1 Timothy 5: 8 says:

> *'But if any provide not for his own, and specially for those of his own house, he hath denied the faith, and is worse than an infidel.'*

Isn't it amazing that the Word of God covers all aspects of our lives. The Word is lamp unto our feet. It shows us the way. In a situation where the man and his wife both have jobs and the man's salary is not enough to pay for every bill, the woman can support with a supplementary income. If all that the man's salary can pay for is the rent and food, it is ideal that he does that. Now the woman can support by paying for the other bills. As his help, she supports in any area that lack exists, but when it comes to the provision of food and shelter, the man should stand up to it. There is something about the man taking responsibility of these two important things, food and shelter. It keeps him in charge, and it causes the woman to be more submissive because she feels loved, secured, and provided for. On the contrary, if the woman takes on this responsibility, then there has been a switch of roles and before long she will seem to be the head of the family because she carries the major responsibilities. It is unnatural for the woman to be the leader in the home; the family will be disorganised. However, she could be a leader at her place of work or in organisation with other men, but she would never assume the role of being a leader or head in the home. The devil could use that as an opportunity to tempt her. I have seen some families where the man takes on all the financial responsibilities and allows his wife to keep whatever money she gets for herself. The men that do that do it with a mentality of a head. In such homes, you find peace and love reigning.

I will also like to say that it isn't the plan of God for you to experience lack. In previous chapters we've seen that there is a good life prearranged by God for his children (Eph. 2: 10). That life is free from struggle; it is a life that comes with provision. God declared in his Word that those that have entered into his rest have seized from their struggles (Heb. 4: 10). Just as God has entered his own rest and has ceased from his works; this means that you do everything, whether business or ministry, from a position of rest. Your whole life has been arranged before you came, therefore go back to God in prayer and remain at that place of prayer until he reveals to you his plans concerning you, not your own plans. Whether it is career, business etc. when you've found out, that's when you will begin to experience true prosperity and peace.

As the Vision Carrier

The man as the head of the family gives a sense of purpose. He brings a vision from God for the family to run with. He lays down the plans God has for the family, and the woman helps this vision come true. Chris does that in our home. At the beginning of every year, Chris would tell me about his plans for the family, and then we present it to the Lord in prayers, but we found out that we are unable to carry out those plans; we finally discovered that we ought to pray for God's plan and purpose for our family instead of our own plans. At that point, everything changed; we began to experience true peace and purpose. Vision could help to strengthen marriages because the couple will have a sense of purpose thereby working together as a team to achieve a common goal. It will promote a sense of oneness. Vision sharing in the family takes away unnecessary rivalry and promotes oneness. When a woman clearly understands what the vision is, she adjusts herself where necessary to ensure that that vision comes to pass. But if the man hasn't gotten any vision, the woman being the closest person to him, knowing his strengths and his God-given talents, could help him in finding it, through prayers. Remember, the woman is a help to the man.

Prayer

Dear heavenly father, there is none beside you. Thank you for crowning me with your glory and making me the head of my family. Help me to be uncompromisingly submitted to you so that I can be an effective leader. I understand now all that my responsibilities are as the head of the family. I know that I can do all things through Christ that strengthens me. By your wisdom I will deal wisely with every member of my family. May I head my home to your glory even as Christ heads the church, in Jesus name. Amen

Chapter Six

The Role of a Christian Woman

When God said to Adam 'I will make you a helper suitable', he meant someone who will stand by you to help you achieve all your dreams, someone to share responsibilities with. The woman is the assistant manager in the home. In all that the man is called to do, she is that vital ingredient that makes it work. A dear man of God once told me that the only two personalities described in the Bible as helpers is the ***Holy Spirit*** and the ***woman.*** How true that is. Her role in marriage is as follows:

Being Submissive

The issue of submission has become a major topic of debate in the church today. Some say the submission is a mutual one rather than one-sided. Others claim that the submission is the sole responsibility of the wife. The truth of the matter is this; the submission is actually a mutual one because if a man loves his wife unconditionally as Christ loves the church and died for her, that man is actually submitted to her as in his service to her, but she submits to his leadership as the head. The Bible says the glory of a woman is her husband, and the glory of the man is God. With the man as the head the woman is to submit to his leadership. What kind of a woman would not submit to a husband that loves her with the last breath of his life? A woman's submission to her husband is actually a duty she renders to the Lord. And a husband's submission is a service he owes his wife, but both of them are accountable to God. The Scripture does not imply that she submits to every man but to her own husband in the same way that the church is subject to Christ (Eph. 5: 22-24). She submits by allowing him to rule over her, yielding her will for his. There might be a difference in opinion concerning issues, but both parties must come to a compromise in love. The only time that a woman can be excused is when her husband is asking her to do something that is against the Word of God.

Sarah called Abraham Lord, not because he was her god but rather she was acknowledging his authority over her. A woman's obedience to God's Word can transform an unbelieving husband to the obedience of Christ (1 Pet. 3: 7).

Humility is the key to being submissive. When the woman is humble, it is easy for her to submit because God will give her the grace. Bible declares that God resists the proud and gives grace to the humble. A woman is not only expected to submit her will, but also her body to her own husband.

As a Home Keeper

Apart from being submissive to her husband, she has the sole responsibility of running the home, and that involves caring for the children, cooking, cleaning, etc. Looking at the Proverb 31 woman, we see that she is not idle; she has a lot going on all at the same time. Her effectiveness in running her home brought praise to her husband. Bible records that her children rise up and call her blessed. Some people say that it's not possible for anyone to be like her in real sense. Don't be deceived, it is very possible. God has given to the woman grace to fulfil her role. No one sends a labourer into the farm without tools to get the job done. In any assignment that God gives you, there is unction to function. There is an anointing on the Christian wife to perform in her role. A woman has the ability of doing many things at the same time just as we see the Proverbs 31 woman, but a man can only do one at a time. We have five young children at home, I do the household chores though the kids are a bit grown up now to help, but the onus is still on me. I'm not saying it's very easy with five kids that have never gone to a childminder, but what I'm saying is that God himself strengthens us to do, by his spirit. There are times when I feel I can't carry on any longer, my strength had failed. At such times I begin to talk to the Lord, asking and receiving grace, and suddenly I feel an inner strength within me causing me to go ahead. Grace is available; all we need to do is receive it. The way to receive anything from God is by faith through our confession. Just say I receive grace to carry out this task (name it) in Jesus name. When you say that, believe that you have received it and you shall have it (Mark 11: 24). One of the ministries of the Holy Spirit is to strengthen us so that we can reach our full potentials.

The primary assignment of the woman, given by God is the home. If she feels capable of taking on a second job outside the home, it's her own decision, but it should not be at the detriment of her God-given job. We have already seen that God established the family structure for the purpose of raising godly men and women. Now let me ask you this, if the woman also goes out to work every day like her husband, and the children spend their days in school and after that at the childminder's, Monday to Friday, and then spend two days in the week, Saturdays and Sundays with their parents, sincerely answer the question, who has raised those children, is it the society or the parents? Obviously, the one that spends more time with the children has more influence over them. We have seen and heard that children carry guns to school and shoot their fellows. What happened, what is troubling them inside? Where did we miss it? Is it really true that we have abandoned the traditional Christian family system and have embraced modern societal lifestyle? The answer is yes. As mothers, we should spend time with the children, teaching them the Word of God at home at least twice a week apart from church. If we can help them with their home work every day, we can also take out twenty minutes twice in the evenings to teach them God's Word. You'll be amazed how much of the Word they'll have inside them as they grow up. I saw the lane which our Christian children are travelling on before I decided to start a home Bible study with my children. Though they were born in the church, they had little or no knowledge of the Word. I decided to ask them some simple Bible quiz, but to my greatest surprise they could not even name all twelve disciples of Jesus, but they knew all Beyonce's music off heart. That frightening realisation drove me into teaching them the Word during the week, just like I help with their school homework. If you have not yet started teaching your children at home, I encourage you to begin today. Always pray for them and with them. Don't leave it all to the pastor because they are your primary responsibility.

She Must Respect Her Husband

It is indeed a virtue for a woman to respect her husband. Esteem your husband; it doesn't matter whether you feel he deserves it or not. Let this mind be in you that your husband is your priority, and often let him know that nothing is more important to you than him. The reason is that he is your glory. The Bible says that the glory of the woman is her husband. Your beauty is your husband, without him you are incomplete. When he offends you, learn to separate the offence from his person. By so doing, you'll find out that instantaneous forgiveness is possible. This could be more understood when you look back to Jesus's teaching about offence and forgiveness. Peter asked him how many times one could forgive. Jesus said seven times seventy. This means you forgive as often as you are offended.

Respecting your husband also means that you shouldn't be a nagging wife. No man wants to be with a woman who nags him. Proverbs 25: 24 says:

> *'It is better to dwell in the corner of the housetop, than with a brawling woman and in a wide house.'*

If you have any concerns, both of you could sit down and talk about it. As a Christian wife, you must pursue peace. If he won't change any bad attitudes that brings strive in the home, then you have to summon him to heaven's court by praying to the Father, and he, the Father of peace, will speak and calm all the storms in your marriage. If you try to force him or manipulate to have things your way, it then means that you've left your place of being submissive. A man will oppose a woman that wants to be equal with him; he'll begin to see you as an opponent and not a wife. Nagging causes a woman's attractiveness to her husband to depreciate. A man finds comfort in the arms of his wife when challenges come to him, but a nagging wife chases him away.

Now, I know it can be very frustrating when your husband refuses to take charge of situations as the head of the house. You've done all that you could to make him see reasons, but all to no avail. If you are in this kind of situation, do not despair; be encouraged by the Word of God. He said, when your obedience is complete, he will bring down that disobedience that has come to trouble you (Isa. 1: 1-2, 2 Cor. 10: 6, emphasis added). Don't stop being submissive just because your husband has an attitude problem, because it is God that has commanded you through his Word to be submissive.

So when you're not submissive, it is actually God that you've resisted and disobeyed. Let me illustrate this point even further, if you assault or disobey a police officer, even if he had mistreated you, you have not only insulted that particular officer, but also the authority that backs him up. That includes the commissioner of police and the minister of justice. At that point, it is the state that will go after you until you pay the penalty of that crime. So you see that complete submission to any authority is very important. Submit to your husband's authority and you will be submitting to God's. The Word of God, through your selfless prayers, will change your husband. God loves your marriage; he has sanctified it. Since you got married in obedience to his Word, his name is on your marriage. He is interested in every detail of your marriage. Just keep being a doer of God's Word.

She Prays for Her Husband

We pray for our leaders, we pray for our pastors, we ought also to pray for our husbands. One thing is common among these categories of people. They are all leaders in their different offices.

When a woman begins to pray for her husband, her prayers help to keep him focused. There are many things out there seeking his attention, but the prayers will keep him on course. As the head of the home, it is costly for him to be distracted. You, as a wife, will receive answers when you pray for your husband because you are highly favoured. When you came into your man's life, you came with favour, and the word has confirmed that by saying, 'He that finds a wife finds a good thing and obtains favour from God'.

You are in partnership with the Holy Spirit in helping the man, so begin today to pray for his job, his finances, his business, his ministry, and his relationships. Pray for him to administer all his affairs with wisdom. There may be times when you know that he's going the wrong way about something; if you gently talk and he refuses to adhere, don't nag, don't scream but go down on your knees and pray for him, and you will see a reverse in that situation. There is power in praying for your husband.

I remember one morning Chris woke up feeling moody—he would not speak to me, and it went on like that the whole day. I could not place my hand exactly on what was going on, but I knew he was troubled in his spirit. I decided to take up a fast for him. The next morning, I was in my living room praying for him and commanding the enemy to leave our territory; while I was yet praying, Chris came into the room to talk to me. I realised that even before I said amen his countenance had changed; whatever it was that bothered him had left him. I was so amazed at how quick the prayer worked. That day I learnt this spiritual truth about praying for your spouse. I noticed that my prayers were not selfish, it was all about Chris. I wasn't crying to the Lord that my husband would not speak to me; I didn't ask the Lord for my vindication. I just asked the devil to lose his hold on my husband, and the heaviness left instantly. If I had reacted otherwise, I would have gotten a different result. Like I said earlier, most people find it hard to pray that selfless prayer I talked about, but that's the only way you can break through. You must stand in the gap for your spouse at their down times. Such times includes when they are up against you. Your spouse is not the enemy, so when you find them behaving in a negative way, you must realise that the devil is at work, trying to cause dissension in your home. Don't let it linger for long; address the issues spiritually and fast before it gets the better of you. Go into the realm of the spirit and pick up words of love. Many who find it hard to pray for their husbands are actually responding to their experiences of hurt and not love because the consideration of the experiences of hurt will not let you pray for him. But the meditation of your love will allow you to pray for him because love believes for good in every person.

Prayer

Dear lord, you are my father and you have made me a member of this great family of Christ. Thank you for the opportunity you have given me to be a helper to my husband, through your grace I will build my home and not tear it apart. I have received from you the ability to help my husband in all his endeavours in life. Help me lord to be humble and completely submissive to his leadership in Jesus name. Amen

Chapter Seven

Building a Strife-Free Home

Have you ever wondered about the possibility of having a strife-free marriage? Having a ring around your finger does not bring satisfaction to the heart. Harmonious living is the key. We need to consciously make effort everyday to keep our marriages strong and not let it go towards divorce. How good and pleasant it is for brethren to dwell together in unity (Ps. 133: 1). Be ready to do all things of one accord, of one mind. Let nothing be done through strife or vainglory; you can live in harmony with one another. Philippians 2: 2-3 says:

> *'fulfil ye my joy that ye be likeminded, having the same love, being of one accord, of one mind. Let nothing be done through strife or vainglory; but in lowliness of mind let each esteem the other better than themselves.'*

This Scripture promotes harmonious living; it is the foundation for strife-free living. This Scripture is the result of what we want. Now we will look at various steps to attaining this result. If these things that we are about to examine be in you and abound, they'll make your marriage fruitful and full of joy.

Step 1—Acknowledge Christ Being at the Centre of Your Marriage

There is a God between you and your spouse, and be conscious of that fact, and when you do, God takes the headship in the marriage. The love between David and Jonathan in 1 Samuel 20 was sustained because they had sworn 'the Lord be between me and thee'. Just the same way you swore and took the oath of marriage before the Lord. When this becomes your mindset, the spirit of the fear of the Lord will fill you so much so that you will know how to relate with your spouse in humility and enjoy the bliss of marriage. One remarkable thing about Christ being at the centre of your marriage is that as you draw closer to him individually, you will find yourselves also closer to one another.

Step 2—Having Mutual Respect Towards One Another

Mutual respect stems from self-respect. If you have no respect for yourself, then you have nothing to give. This principle of mutual respect works in all kinds of relationships, not just marriage. If you have respect for yourself, you'll have the ability to respect others. Respecting your spouse is not based solely on how well they perform but rather on love. In our dealings with our spouses it is important that we show consideration for their feelings, and these considerations must be mutual. If you disregard or disrespect your spouse, the result could be a feeling of rejection, embarrassment, and hurt, especially if you disregard them before other people. On the contrary, respecting your spouse will give them a feeling of self-worth, love, and appreciation. Therefore, sow respect and you will reap a harvest of respect.

Four years ago, I cultivated a habit of addressing every married male as 'sir', whether rich or poor, Christian or non-Christian. It was my way of showing respect to them and also for myself. Sometimes, the one I'm greeting looks back as though I was talking to someone else. Before long, I realised that I made people feel important, they felt good about themselves. I remember one summer morning in Nigeria, I met a man who was seeking employment from someone I know. We met at this fellow's house, and I greeted him, addressing him as 'sir'. His reaction was astounding; it was a mixed reaction. He felt so embarrassed that I said that in front of a prospective employer, and at the same time happy to be respected by someone that is wealthier than himself, in spite of his condition. From the look in his eyes I could see his thoughts; it was as though he was saying 'don't blow this opportunity up for me, but you make me feel worthy'. My spirit was elated at how a little word like 'sir' could make someone feel so important. Make up your mind to respect people as well as your spouses, and your deeds will be reciprocated.

Step 3—Exercising Self-Control

The *Oxford English Dictionary* defined self-control as the ability to control one's emotions or behaviour in difficult situations. Self-control means restraining yourself from within. It is actually a virtue that should be sought after like gold. As Christians, we know that the presence of the Holy Spirit in us produces self-control amongst other virtues. What you need do is to practice it. A Christian without self-control is exposed to the fiery missiles of the devil. Proverbs 25: 28 says that:

> *'He that hath no rule over his own spirit is like a city that is broken down and without walls.'*

Isn't that fascinating? A city without walls has no security; it is open for anyone and anything to enter and attack at any time. If you do not have self-control, the devil will come in, and we know that he comes only to kill, to steal and to destroy. His primary purpose is to destroy your marriage if you let him. On the contrary, Proverbs 16: 32 says:

'He that rules his spirit is better than he that takes a city.'

In other words, he that exercises self-control is better than a mighty warrior that is without. It tells us how important it is to have self-control.

A man heard that his wife had been committing adultery; he furiously came back home and pounced on her without first finding out if it was true. He later found out that the story was untrue. He was so sorry, and he wished he could undo the damage, but it obviously was too late. He had called her all the horrible names there is. So you see, the importance of self-control cannot be overemphasised. Make a quality decision to put it to work, even in the face of strong oppositions. There is a saying in Ireland that 'Silence is golden'. How true that is; keeping quiet at turbulent times at home does not make you a fool, rather it means that you are in charge of your emotions. There is always a more excellent way of expressing yourself.

Step 4—Effective Communication

Communication is simply understood as an exchange of information between two or more individuals. But communication is not effective unless there is a clear understanding of what has been communicated. For you to ensure that your spouse understands you, you have to communicate in the language that they understand. Ensure that you are not misunderstood. Avoid assumptions; ask again if you have to, in order to have a clear understanding. If communication between you and your spouse is effective, the goals and aspirations of the family will come true. Same way, God communicates to us through the Bible; our understanding of what he has said makes us either prosperous or poor.

Your background will also play a part in how you communicate with your spouse or with people. Some people grew up in families where communication is by sarcasms or with an intention of ridiculing the other. That attitude may begin to play out in your marriage if you bring it in. Some people's way of communication could be to answer a question with a question, for example, the wife says, 'Jimmy, have you seen my shoe?' His response is, 'Where did you keep it?' Or she says, 'Are you going out?' And he says, 'To where?' If this is your way of communication, how can you reconcile the difference if your spouse's way is different? The right pattern for communication is that of love. You mean what you say and say what you mean.

Transparency is another fundamental ingredient. You must be open with one another so that you can see through each other. Do not withhold any information from each other, no matter how insignificant you feel it is. Let your spouse know what you are about. Make decisions together.

Step 5—Keeping Godly Friends

The Bible advices us to keep company with godly people, especially true Christians. I deliberately chose the word 'true' because there are some in the church who are still carnal; they are ruled by their senses, and their judgements are based on how they feel and by what they see or hear. Your marital issues should be kept from such folks because their advice to you could cause more harm than good. Go with God-fearing people—people who will hold hands with you and pray, people who will rebuke you when you're wrong, those who have understanding of the word. They rejoice with you when you rejoice and they cry with you when you cry, bearing one another's burdens and celebrating Christ. Consider the life of Job; when he was going through those strong challenges in his life, Satan could not make him renounce God, but when he started reasoning with his three friends, Eliphaz, Bildad, and Sophar, who examined his situation and gave him wrong counsel, he began to question God as though God had been unfaithful to him. None of Job's friends sought God on his behalf concerning the tragedy that had befallen him, but they blamed him constantly for his predicaments. Watch what God says about those who fear him in Malachi 3: 16-17, amplified version.

> *'Then those who feared the lord talked often one to another; and the lord listened and heard it, and a book of remembrance was written before Him of those who reverenced and worshipfully feared the lord and who thought on His name. And they shall be mine, says the lord of host, in that day when I publicly recognize and openly declare them to be my jewels, my special possession, my peculiar treasure. And I will spare them as a man spares his own son who serves him.'*

Would you love to be among this people that the almighty God is making this solemn declaration about? I know that some have had bad experiences in the church, and this is sad, but there are still true worshippers. Search diligently for Christians like this and make friends with them. You will experience true fellowship, and your relationship with God will become more intimate. Your knowledge of God's Word also will be on the increase everyday as you communicate with each other and share the testimonies of God's goodness. Your relationship with these kinds of friends will help your marriage stay strong because of accountability.

On the other hand, discussing your marital affairs with unbelieving friends and family members is even more dangerous because there is a high risk of you being influenced negatively. It's not just who you talk to, but also who you hang out with. 1 Corinthians 15: 33 says evil communication corrupts good manners. Notice, it doesn't read, evil communication corrupts good communication, but it affects your manners, your lifestyle, and your attitude. Your association with unbelievers will deprave the good habits that you have cultivated through the Word of God. A certain young man formed the habit of going out for a drink every Friday with his colleagues at work. At first it seemed harmless but after a while, his attitude at home began to change, and he became a bit nonchalant, he'll yell at the kids unnecessarily and showed no respect to his wife. According to his wife, she realised he had started acting and sounding like one particular friend among the group that he hangs out with. This alien behaviour provoked all kinds of problems. They fight about one thing today and the next day it's another. That marriage today is at the verge of falling apart because of wrong influence.

It is necessary that we choose the right friends. As a Christian, your old friends and acquaintances are not your enemies but you have become a light to them, a sign post leading them to Christ.

When an unbeliever hears you talk well of your spouse, and if they perceive that you are really in love, either one of two things will happen, they may seek to emulate you, or they may get jealous and try to bring you back to your old life before you became a Christian. Refuse to keep bad company, refuse to be influenced by the circumstances around you. Lift your banner high for Jesus.

Step 6—Love and Sex

How close to you and your spouse in terms of your sexual relations? Those moments of intimacy can bring pure joy and pleasure to your lives. It gives you a sense of fulfilment. Sex connects the body and soul of two as one. This is the reason why God said 'the two shall be one flesh'. It is indeed a beautiful gift from God. A couple that have a healthy sexual relationship will also have enough strength within them to face every challenge that comes against them. Do not allow anything come between your relationship with your spouse. Some are fond of using the children as an excuse. Remember that your children will not always be with you, and they will grow up and eventually get married and leave you. If your relationship with your spouse has already broken down, what happens to both of you after the children leave? You may no longer find satisfaction in that relationship that has become sour and boring, at that stage two things will be knocking at your door; infidelity or divorce. So whatever happens, keep the flames of love burning so that at your later ages you will still be content with one another.

The lack of sufficient sex in a relationship could cause psychological imbalance; frustration, anxiety, and low self-esteem. There is no rule as to how often it should happen, but studies have shown that couples who have sex almost every day live happier and stay closer to each other than those with lesser frequency. You can engage in sexual intercourse as often as the need arises. Bible admonishes that we do not deprive one another except for the sole purpose of prayer so that we do not get tempted. So, do not deprive one another, make no excuses, and make those moments special by spicing it up.

Here Are Some Tips

When you notice that a need for it has risen, prepare for it, make the environment seducing by using scented candles, and low lights instead of the archaic way of being in the dark. You could also have a touch of a soft perfume on your pillows to get that sweet smell oozing out from time to time. Be adventurous; don't remain under a particular pattern. It pays off at the long run. Make out time to spend alone with one another, away from the hustle and bustle of life. No matter what happens, don't stop dating each other. Go out together as you did during your courtship; agree between yourselves to talk about nothing else but yourselves; no talk about your financial challenges, and don't talk about your problems with your mother-in-law, it could ruin your evening. Just go out and enjoy yourselves. If you're not financially buoyant, you could still go out for a walk in the cool of the day and enjoy each other's company.

Form the habit of surprising one another with gifts; it doesn't have to be expensive but nice. Wastefully pour love into one another as if pouring water into a vessel until it overflows. No matter what happens, keep the flames of love burning, and don't let the coals quench. Remember to send text messages of love to one another; you could write a lovely note and put in her purse or in his wallet; hug each other often without sexual intentions.

This beautiful gift of sex has one golden rule and God demands that this rule be not broken. If the rule breaks, it causes pain, guilt, and unforgiveness, and in some cases sickness and death. The rule of sex is this; it should be between two married people. You are not allowed by God to have multiple sex partners. Proverbs 6: 32-33 says:

> *'But whoso committeth adultery with a woman lacketh understanding: he that doeth it destroyeth his own soul.'*

And the result in verse 33 is dishonour and shame.

Quite often, people who have cheated in their marriage did not do it intentionally. They were just at the wrong place at the wrong time, or hanging around with wrong folks. Even if you are born again, if you expose yourself and go to places where your old sin nature can be aroused, you will be burnt. It doesn't matter how spiritual you are, if you go to the wrong place you will fall. Don't trust your flesh; no good thing is in the flesh; to be carnally minded is death.

Sexual immorality is a tool that Satan uses today to fight against the church. We have heard of great men and women who have been brought down by this sin. It cuts through every stratum. It is not a respecter of persons. Sexual immorality does not just happen; the idea is first conceived in the mind, the mind processes the thought, and then the actual sin takes place. If you are attracted to someone other than your spouse, I will advice that you expose it by confessing it to your spouse before it gets the better of you. At that stage you have not sinned, and what you feel is an external force trying to infest or attack your mind. It is only when you begin to process the thoughts that conception takes place, and sin when it is fully conceived brings forth death. So, as you confess it, it loses its power over you. There is power release in confession. Never assume that if you confess to your spouse that you feel attracted to someone, then they will be mad at you. On the contrary, your honesty and sincerity shows that you don't intend to cheat and that you need help.

If you have a weakness in this area and you sincerely want to stop, first you must know that you cannot stop on your own; you need God's help because it is a spiritual battle, the flesh fighting to own your will and gain the mastery over you, and your spirit also fighting to uphold God's law. But remember that if you are a Christian, you are a new creature in Christ, and the law of the spirit of life in Christ has made you free from the law of sin and death, so sin cannot have dominion over you. It means if you fight against it, you will win.

'For the weapons of our warfare are not carnal but they are mighty through God to the pulling down of strong holds, casting down imaginations and every high thing that exalts itself against the knowledge of God, and bringing into captivity every thought to the obedience of Christ.'

Wow! What a weapon! So effective it will pull down that strong hold in your life. The spirit of immorality will flee from you as you make use of our spiritual weapons.

Go to the Bible and get out all the Scriptures that talk about this subject; pray and meditate on the word; as you do, visualise our weapons smashing down every strong hold or thought in your life. Then begin to speak faith-filled words, I bet you those walls will fall down flat.

Step 7—Be Disciplined with Words

Words could uplift a person, and words could bring them down. A person could appreciate or depreciate in value to you depending on the kind of words you use on them. If you use negative words, after a while the person loses value in your sight, but if you use positive words, that person will begin to mean more to you. Words have power to either bring peace or war. The world as we see it today is framed by words; God spoke the Word and it was so. The words you speak could either bring life or death to your marriage (Prov. 18: 21). Words are like eggs, once they fall to the ground, you can never put them back together again. When you use wrong words on your partner, it's not only that it hurts, but they never forget about it even if they have forgiven you. A good man out of his good treasure of the heart brings forth good things, and an evil man out of the evil treasure brings forth evil things (Matt. 12: 35). Let your treasure be full of God's Word so that you will bring forth good fruits. The same mouth you use for love should not be used for curse, after all sweet and bitter waters does not come from the same source (James 3: 11).

Each time, I remember my childhood years, I remember all the nice words that were spoken to me by my parents, and they still make me feel good about myself, and the 'not so good' words also brings a negative reflection of the past. I would often wish that I never heard them.

The Prophet Isaiah said in chapter 50: 4

> *'The lord hath given me the tongue of the learned that I should know how to speak a word in season to him that is weary . . .'*

When you speak a word to a weary soul, it soothes and brings comfort and encouragement. In Ephesians 4: 29, the Bible also admonishes us thus:

> *'Let no corrupt communication proceed out of your mouth, but only that which is good to the use of edifying, that it may minister grace unto the hearers.'*

Do your words encourage and strengthen your spouse? Or do they bring about strive? Proverbs 25: 11 says:

> *'A word fitly spoken is like apples of gold in pictures of silver.'*

Gentle words could turn away rage; it could make your spouse's heart tender towards you. If you have been using the wrong words, decide today to change, decide that your mouth will only speak words of blessing. Always choose the right words, words of encouragement, words of love, words that bring hope to the hearer, words of praise, and words of appreciation.

Step 8—Avoid Emotional Blow-Ups

Anger is the expression of negative emotions. Anger could be expressed in two distinct ways—through hash words or through polite and controlled words. If your anger is expressed politely, it will cause the subject of your anger to be empathetic and that person could really understand your reason of being angry and feel sorry for hurting you. On the other hand, if you use hash words, they'll cause negative effects. It is natural for all human to feel angry, but the Bible warns us not to sin in our anger, and don't let the sun go down upon your anger. It means that it is possible to be angry without sinning, and also not be angry for long (Eph. 4: 26). Anger has effects on both you and the one you're angry with. Medical science has proved that anger causes an increased heart rate, high blood pressure, and many more health conditions. Have you ever asked your spouse how they feel when you're angry? Obviously, they'll feel unhappy, confused, and even depressed. Anger will make you look unpleasant to your spouse and people around you. There will be no peace around an angry person. Proverbs 11: 29 says:

> *'He that troubles his own household shall inherit the wind . . .'*

Avoid emotional blow-ups and practice patience. Anger can cause an emotional shutdown between you and your spouse. The God kind of love puts up with anything, with the help of the Holy Ghost. I know the question in your heart right now is what are we supposed to do when we are hurt? Your spouse may unintentionally hurt you from time to time, no doubts about that, but when you are hurt, you must respond in love. There is something about anger that many Christians do not know; anger is contagious. If you spend time around a person who is always angry, sooner or later you will be like that also. We know this from God's Word in Proverbs 22: 24-25 says:

> *'Make no friendship with an angry man; and with a furious man thou shall not go: lest thou learn his ways, and get a snare to thy soul.'*

So you see that the effect of anger hinges on people that associate with you as well.

Finally, Ephesians 4: 31-32 admonishes thus, 'let all bitterness, and wrath, and anger, and clamour, and evil speaking be put away from you, with all malice: and be ye kind to one another, tender hearted, forgiving one another, even as God for Christ sake hath forgiven you.'

Step 9—Learn to Appreciate One Another

Appreciation simply means to be grateful and thankful for something. Are you thankful for the things that your spouse does for you? If your answer is yes, then often let them know and don't assume that they already know. They need to hear you say it.

When you have been in a relationship for so long, it's easy to start taking each other for granted. A person whose efforts are appreciated will be willing to do more, and the lack of appreciation could cause disappointment and discouragement, causing your relationship to regress. If you are ungrateful by murmuring and complaining about people that are helping you, sooner or later you will be left alone.

Start now to appreciate your spouse and people around you, make it a habit to say thank you for every kindness shown to you. The mum that manages the home and the dad that works hard to meet the family needs both needs to be appreciated. There are different ways to say thank you. The best way is to say it and put a smile on your spouse's face, letting them know how much they mean to you. However, you could send him or her a thank you card or little gifts.

Make a quality decision to live a life of gratitude.

Step 10—Avoid Jealousy and Insecurity

Jealousy, as defined by the *Oxford Dictionary* is a disposition to suspect rivalry or unfaithfulness. I would say that jealousy is an expression of negative emotions. It arises both in men and women, but most common in women. Havelock Ellis described jealousy as that dragon which slays love under the pretence of keeping it alive. The stories we hear and the movies we watch beclouds our judgements and creates distrust in our relationships as we see and read about how couples cheat and betray each other's trust. This is one of the effects of media on marriages. It creates an unnecessary exposure to sin. Therefore, spend more time in the Word of God and less time in worldly movies and magazines because what you spend more time doing will influence your life more.

If your spouse has given you a reason to doubt their love for you, either through lies or infidelity, it will be naturally difficult to trust them again; but remember unconditional love, see them the way God sees us when we miss it and ask for his forgiveness. Don't allow yourself go through the motions of jealousy because its effects in a relationship are detrimental.

Apart from the fact that jealousy creates distrust in marriages, it also makes the jealous partner feel inadequate and insecure. In Genesis, Cain killed Abel as a result of jealousy; it could tear your marriage apart. One of the signs of jealousy is that it makes you question your spouse over and over again concerning anything, makes you suspicious of their every move, who they talk to and where they've been at. It gives you unnecessary heart pain and unhappiness because there is this pressure in you to perform and meet up with that false sense of inadequacy. If your spouse has given you a reason to doubt their love and commitment towards you, being jealous and suspicious is not the solution. The solution is forgiveness, love, and building trust again. If you have truly forgiven your spouse, then receive the grace to put the issue behind you and move on. Once you have forgiven your spouse, consciously build trust again in the relationship and avoid being resentful. Resentment will not allow the hurt to heal.

There is another kind of jealousy that is most common in men. It is the fear of having a successful wife. Most men tend to be jealous if there wife has more recognition than they, for any reason. If she earns more than they or preferred in ministry, it becomes a problem in disguise. Even her spiritual gifts might become a threat to him. It's not that he doesn't want her to function in the body of Christ, but he fears that he might be relegated. He wants to be her boss anytime and anywhere. Some marriages end in divorce because of this kind of jealousy. This attitude is ungodly. When a man marries a wife, he obtains favour from God. The wife comes into his life with so many blessings. And all these blessings are attributed to him. All of her is his and vice versa. As father does not feel insecure about his son's success, so also a husband should not feel insecure about his wife's success. It all belongs to him. Love is never envious or boils over with jealousy.

Step 11—Forgive and Forget

Complete forgiveness is something a lot of Christians struggle with, perhaps because of the extent of hurt that was done to them. Some say, 'I have forgiven her, but I will never forget what she did to me'. Forgiveness is not complete until you forget about the issue. Each time you talk about the evil done to you in the past, it's like opening up an old wound which will cause it to bleed again. Unforgiveness has caused a lot of divorces in the church. You cannot change anything about the past by resentment, but you can do something about the future.

Colossians 3: 13 says, 'Forbearing one another, and forgiving one another, if any man has a quarrel against any: even as Christ forgave you so also do ye'. The Scripture reveals that forgiveness is not optional, rather it is compulsory. You could be justified to hold on to that anger or the offence that was done against you. You have been hurt, and anyone that hears your story sympathises with you. Yes, but know this, just as you hold on to that offence, it also holds on to you, thereby enslaving you. Remember that you are the one carrying that grievance and nursing it in your heart, not the one that has hurt you. Your heart is not a settlement for grievances; it is the offspring of life. Therefore, lay a guard over your heart and decide what enters and what doesn't enter.

Forgiveness is akin to humility, and unforgiveness is akin to pride. A heart that is humble to the Spirit of God easily forgives, knowing that it also receives forgiveness from the Lord. On the contrary, a proud heart will refuse to forgive even though God hath forgiven him of his own offences. Receiving forgiveness from the Lord is one of the graces of God. Bible says he gives more grace to the humble but the proud he resists (James 4: 6).

One of Jesus' parables in the book of Mathew chapter 18:21 was about a servant who owed his master a lot of money and could not pay back. The servant went to the master and asked for forgiveness for his debt, the master then decided to show him mercy by cancelling his debts. Now, this same servant left his master's presence and met a fellow servant who owes him even less, in spite of his plea the servant who hath just been forgiven of his own debt refused to forgive his fellow servant. The news of what had happened got to the master, and the master was so furious; he called his servant wicked and ungrateful, and revoked his decision to cancel the servant's debt. So much to learn from that story, we must comfort others with the same comfort that we have received.

Like I mentioned in earlier chapter, your spouse is not just your marriage partner, but he or she is also your brother or sister in the Lord so treat them as such so that the enemy does not have anything on you. Decide to forgive even before your forgiveness is asked.

Step 12—Confess Your Faults

The life of a Christian is a life of humility and love. You must be ready and able to acknowledge and admit your fault and to sincerely apologise to one another. James 4: 16 says:

'Confess your faults one to another and pray for one another, that you may be healed. The effectual fervent prayer of the righteous availeth much.'

Here we see confession, prayer and healing, embracing one another. As you confess your fault to your spouse and pray for one another, it provokes healing in your marriage, in your body, and in your souls. As if that is not enough, James goes on to give us background information, letting us know that the prayer of the righteous makes tremendous power available, dynamic in its working (AMP).

Some couples find it difficult to say sorry and admit their faults. Your apology helps your partner forgive you easily without holding back. A husband that thinks that saying sorry to his wife when he offends is a sign of weakness, has missed it all together, it actually shows his strength as a man and a leader and also a true follower of Christ. A man that is unapologetic, who wants to be seen as a strong and a hard man, is actually full of fear and insecurity on the inside.

Step 13—Get Wisdom

Wisdom is the rightful application of knowledge based on God's Word. Wisdom is the Word of God. You need wisdom to have a successful marriage. Proverb 4: 7 says:

'Wisdom is the principal thing; therefore get wisdom: and with all thy getting get understanding.'

God's wisdom will teach you how to manage your home, your children, and your marriage. Wisdom is profitable to direct (Eccles. 10: 10). It will teach you from within what to say and do at a particular time in a particular circumstance, and as you obey, you will find peace to your souls. Jesus has been made unto us wisdom by

God (1 Cor. 1: 30). Now many do not understand that there are two kinds of wisdom; the first is the wisdom of God and the other is the wisdom of this world. They are very distinct one from the other. The wisdom that unbeliever would apply to his marriage is completely different from that of the believer. The believer is moved by a force from within to do right. The Bible tells us in Isaiah 30: 21:

> *'And thine ears shall hear a word behind thee, saying, this is the way, walk in it, when ye turn to the right hand, and when ye turn to the left.'*

This Scripture is talking about the indwelling of God's Spirit in the human body. It means that the control tower is in your spirit, causing you to do right. Wisdom is a force; it propels you to act right and talk right. If wisdom takes its abode in you, you seize to be ordinary; your uniqueness will be evident to all. In the book of 2 Chronicles, we see a beautiful story about a king called Solomon. He pleased God with his sacrifice, and so God responded by giving him a 'blank check'. God asked Solomon what he would have him to do for him (Solomon). At that point King Solomon knew that God could give him whatsoever he asked; he could have asked for silver and gold; he could have asked for the lives of his father's enemies, but he did not, he rather asked for wisdom. Again God was pleased, not only did God give him wisdom that Solomon had asked, he also blessed him with all material things as well. Wisdom brings with it all other blessings. If you operate with the spirit of wisdom, you will administer all your affairs wisely.

Step 14—Marriage and Finance

Disagreement about finance is one of the major causes of divorce these days. You must be honest with your spouse about financial matters. Make your financial decisions together and allow a certain amount of flexibility in spending. Insufficient funds in a believer's marriage could cause a strain in the marriage relationship if not paid attention to. In God there is always provision. There was provision for Adam before God created him. He was created on the sixth day, after everything else was created. Why was he not created on the first or second day? The reason is that God wanted to put him right at the centre of abundance. There were all kinds of food in the garden: fruits, vegetables, meat, and everything else he would ever need. This was before the fall of Adam. Now considering the finished work of Christ, Christ came to save us and to give us back all that were lost in the garden and much more. So how can we still live in lack as believers? Bible says in 2 Corinthians 8: 9:

> *'For ye know the grace of our Lord Jesus Christ, that, though he was rich, yet for your sakes he became poor, that ye through his poverty might rich.'*

God is a God of super abundance, his riches are inexhaustible. We have an abundance of financial grace. The only way we can access and grow in this financial grace is through sowing and reaping. Your earning is a seed, it is not a means to an end. Learn to sow seed into people's lives and also into the work of ministry, and God will multiply your seed sown. Many think that paying of tithes was abolished in the New Testament. Jesus did not come to abolish the law but to fulfil it. Although we are not under the law but under grace, but tithing is a means that God uses to prosper his children. We that are not under the law pay our tithes not under compulsion but willingly because we love the Lord. In Malachi, God said 'prove me and see if I will not open the windows of heaven and pour out a blessing'. That blessing is an empowerment to produce wealth. Just one blessing from the Lord fills you to an overflow he could give you a good business idea, or bless you in whatever way that pleases him. Brothers and sisters, I will urge you to put your gaze on Jesus, the author and finisher of your faith. Be conscious of the supplier, God, who is able to supply all your needs according to his riches in glory by Christ Jesus. David was conscious of the Lord as his supplier when he said, 'the Lord is my shepherd, I shall not want'. When you have Jesus, you have it all.

Step 15—Add Humour to Your Marriage

As couples, how many times do you joke and laugh together? Laughter is medicinal, and it has curative abilities. It can melt down anger, cure depression, fear, stress, and enhance your relationship positively. Proverbs 17: 22 says that:

'A merry heart does good like medicine.'

God has made us so wonderfully and fearfully. Medical researchers have proven that laughter produces chemicals in our bodies that fight against diseases like cancer and some others. Laughter takes your mind off anger or anything that causes worry in your life. As good as laughter is, it's also contagious, so spread it around your home and experience its effects. Isaiah "12:3"

'With joy shall ye draw out of the wells of salvation.'

The well of salvation is full of divine graces; divine healing is one of God's graces. And remember it does not read 'streams', which runs dry, but it reads 'well'. It means that God's grace is inexhaustible, and joy is the gateway. Praise God. So now that we know the importance of laughter and true joy; begin to practice developing a good sense of humour. You could get a video or a CD of Christian jokes or comedy and enjoy together. Fill your day with moments of laughter.

'Finally, love endures long and is patient and kind; love never is envious nor boils over with jealousy, is not boastful or vainglorious, does not display itself haughtily. It is not conceited, arrogant, and inflated with pride; it is not rude (unmannerly) and does not act unbecomingly. Love (God's love in us) does not insist on its own rights or its own way, for it is not self-seeking; it is not touchy or fretful or resentful; it takes no account of evil done to it (it pays no attention to a suffered wrong). It does not rejoice at injustice or unrighteousness, but rejoices when right and truth prevails. Love bears up under anything and everything that comes; is ever ready to believe the best of every person, its hopes are fadeless under all circumstances, and it endures everything (without weakening). Love never fails (never fades out or becomes obsolete or comes to an end). As for prophesy (the gift of interpreting the divine will and purpose), it will be fulfilled and will pass away; as for tongues, they will be destroyed and cease; as for knowledge, it will pass away (it will lose it power and be superseded by truth). But love never fails' (1 Cor. 13: 4-8, amplified version).

All of these above mentioned steps interplay together. You can do it if you are determined to win in your marriage, and as you decide to adapt these steps in building a strife-free home, the Spirit of the living God will be your help, your counsellor, your strength, and your advocate. You cannot fail because your connection to the Holy Spirit takes away pride, fear, lust and the like, and gives you love, joy, and a sound mind.

Prayer

Father, you are the God of peace. Thank you for your word that lets me know the immense benefit of living a life of peace. It pleases you that your children dwell together in unity and peace. May Christ be at the centre of my marriage. Through the love and peace that I express outwardly, my family and friends will see Christ in me in Jesus name. Amen

Chapter Eight

Marriage and Divorce

Divorce has become one of the strongest challenges facing the body of Christ today. It is indeed a tragedy. Divorce rate among Christians is on the increase, even ministers of the Gospel of whom the church is looking up to are getting divorced, and I don't mean that critically. It's the truth. The older generation had less cases of divorce in the church than this present generation. The reason for this is that they did not have the 'I can't take it anymore' mentality. They had the 'we can work it out' mentality. So when they were faced with challenges in their marriages, they endured and were willing and ready to find solutions based on God's Word. They had a clear understanding of their roles, and they respected their uniqueness. In this generation, if we can understand clearly the meaning and purpose of this great union called marriage, not through the light of the world, their ideas and opinions about marriage, but through the light of God's Word, then we will also understand that there is no way out of it.

Divorce is almost unheard of among Christians who are going through persecution. If you go to China or the Muslim countries where Christians are being persecuted, you will realise that their priorities are different; they are busy finding out new ways of spreading the

Gospel, and if they are caught, they are ready to die for the sake of this Gospel that you and I freely enjoy. You don't hear them talking about divorce, or see them take themselves to court. A dear brother visited our church from China, while he testified of God's goodness towards the saints amidst the persecutions, the whole church was silent. He told of how they meet in cells, and how they would not clap their hands loud in praise to the Lord because someone might hear and report them to the authorities, yet the Gospel is burning like fire in their bones. They have no freedom to evangelise openly, yet they risk their lives everyday making disciples for Jesus. At the end of that service, we all went home with one question burning in our hearts and that is, what can we also do for Jesus? Brothers and sisters thank God for the liberty we enjoy, but should we take our liberty in Christ for granted? Is it the same Bible we read with this, Brethen? This is a provoking thought, and I pray it provokes us to have a rethink about this so-called liberty we have. Galatians 5: 13 states, 'For brethren, ye have been called unto liberty; only use not liberty for an occasion to the flesh, but by love serve one another'. I mean if we use the same Bible as they do and have the same Holy Spirit then why are they so spiritually minded, while we are busy divorcing one another? The reason is that they are not materialistic; they have allowed the word to teach them that indeed the world belongs to them, so there is no use fighting to get what already belongs to them. They have completely surrendered themselves to the Spirit of God without any reservation. Their greatest concern is to spread the Gospel. They do have the choice of relocating to a country whose laws are liberal, but they choose to stay back and spread the Gospel. Apostle Paul counts the suffering that he went through as dung that he may win Christ.

The system and principles of this world is contrary to the principles of God's kingdom, but if we act as they do, then what is the difference between us and them? We must be different so that we may be the children of our Father in heaven (Matt. 5: 45-47). The Word of God is lamp unto our feet and a light unto our path. Marriage is meant to last forever. It lives as long as the both parties live. The only way that marriage could be broken is if one party dies. When God instituted marriage he did not include an exit door, divorce is not in God's original plan. Nothing can quench love. Ecclesiastes 8: 7 says:

> *'That deep waters can't quench love nor flood sweep it away.'*

If it is a true love, an unconditional love, troubles and challenges cannot quench the love that reigns in your marriage neither can the temptations, except you let them. Don't let the devil tear your family apart, if you stand hand in hand with one another, in one voice, you will surely win. There is nothing the devil can do about it. The church cannot be intimidated by the tricks of the devil; we are a victorious church.

The God kind of love that you have in you does not deny wrong doing, but because it is an 'in spite of' love, it is ready to suffer wrong knowing that God will surely rescue. I know that the Word of God says divorce is permissible if any of the party commits adultery. That was under the law. Jesus lived under the law to fulfil it; he died that we might be free from the law and live under the grace of God. For no one could keep the law and obtain righteousness. Our righteousness under the law is like a filthy rag before the Lord. A filthy rag is useless because it's already filthy, and it has no further use. That is self-righteousness as God sees it. The law was supposed to be a schoolmaster to the people of God, guiding them and showing them the way, but they could not keep it; it was now like a stumbling block to them, showing them what sin was. As Christians, we live under grace; we cannot be justified under the law. Now that we are under Christ, the grace of God, shouldn't we rather forgive that wrong done to us than breaking this great union? Jesus said it is permissible because of the hardness of the heart of man. He knew if he had said to forgive adultery, the people will reject his message completely and even stone him.

Mary Magdalene was caught in the very act of adultery. What was Jesus' response when she was brought to him? He likened the sin of adultery to any other sin. He said, 'If you have no sin cast the first stone'. They all knew they had skeletons in there cupboards. You know how the story ended; Jesus did not condemn her, but he let her go free, without a charge. Mercy prevailed over judgement. Hallelujah. Indeed the grace of God hath appeared unto all men.

Remember, we are talking about an unconditional love. Most people feel that the only way to be happy again after they've been hurt is through divorce, that's untrue; one could leave a marriage because the circumstances have become intolerable only to get to the next marriage and be faced with similar or totally new kind of problems. It shows the imperfections in man. Christ is our perfection. If we allow Christ to live his life in us, we will gradually grow into his perfection. Again, divorce is not the way out; complete forgiveness is the way to be happy again.

It was not God's plan for marriages to break, in the beginning it wasn't so. In Mathew 19, when Jesus was asked a question about divorce, his answer to them was that it was not of God to divorce (paraphrased).

'And Jesus answered and said unto them, have ye not read, that he which made them at the beginning made them male and female, and said, for this cause shall a man leave his father and mother and shall cleave to his wife; and they twain shall be one flesh? Wherefore they are no more twain but one flesh. What therefore God hath joined together, let not man put asunder.'

If you examine this Scripture again, you'll see that there is something about the twain becoming one flesh. He could say the twain shall be ***as*** one, but rather he said the twain shall be one flesh, a definite article. It therefore means that they will be inseparable, two souls under one flesh, united and with one voice. If this is true, how then can one flesh become separable? The man after marriage should no longer see himself as separate from the woman; whatever he does to the woman he had done to himself, likewise the woman. Jesus finishes up that Scripture by saying no man should put asunder what God hath joined together. It means that what divinity hath put together let humanity not put asunder. It is sad enough that Christians get divorced, but they, the heirs of salvation, walk down to court and stand before unbelieving pagan judges and allow them to put asunder what the almighty God has joined together is something the whole Christendom should mourn about. Think about this, an atheist who happens to be a judge pronounces divorce over two Christians seeking to be separated thereby cancelling God's Word over their lives; being satisfied with his judgement, they forsake the word of their God and abide by the word of this unbeliever. We allow a mere mortal to cancel God's Word over our lives. This is exactly what we are doing; we are making a mockery of our God. The Bible says that we will judge the world, not the world to pass judgement on us. We are the hope of the world; we have the solutions to the problems of this world. Why then do we act as though we are of the world?

Our Lord, Jesus, before he went into glory taught his disciples. He said love your enemies, bless them that curse you, do good to them that hate you, and pray for them which despitefully use you, that you may be children of your Father in heaven. This teaching shows that our response to matters of life is completely different to the world's way. If we act as they do, what will distinguish us from them? We live by the principles of God's Word. In Romans 8: 19, the Bible shows us how important we are in the world. It says:

> *'For the earnest expectation of the creature waiteth for the manifestation of the sons of God.'*

We are the ones the whole world is waiting to see, the sons of God. We cannot imbibe the ways of this world; we have been chosen out of this world by our Lord Jesus. The world itself is depending on us to change things; we rub the world of the opportunity to see God's glory if we do not manifest our sonship. Why should we join them and act like children of the world. Jesus, in Mathew 7, said we are the salt of the world; if we lose our savour, how can our saltiness be restored. The reality of the kingdom of God must dawn in our spirit. Then only would we begin to live according to the prescribed order in the kingdom. The sufferings of this present time are not worthy to be compared with the glory, which shall be revealed in us; therefore, we must endure hardship in whatever way it comes, as good soldiers of Christ. These days, most churches have accepted divorce amongst believers; they even have programmes designed to help couples go through divorce. It saddens the heart of the Father that the church's silence about divorce is encouraging more believers to have divorce. We must admit that divorce is a tragedy and it is destroying our children; the pain of divorce goes in so deep in the inside of our hearts causing so much tears and fear.

The Tools of Satan

Divorce is one of the tools of Satan to frustrate the believer. As I said earlier, he tries to oppose all that God loves. And God loves marriage, so the enemy tries to corrupt this holy union. He has subtly introduced same sex marriage, fornication, adultery, and prostitution.

All this sexual sins are targeted to destroy or annul God's original plan of marriage. Sexual immorality is a perversion of the truth. Our bodies are the temple of God, and the enemy lures people into sexual immorality just to defile them. When Jesus was on earth, he was tempted in every way but yet without sin. He upheld the integrity of the kingdom till the end; he was never found acting contrary to his teachings. He fulfilled his assignment through the help of the Holy Ghost, and that very same spirit has been given to the church. If we walk in the spirit, we will not gratify the desires of the flesh.

Are we yielding ourselves completely to him? Let us not make God seem unfaithful; he abides faithful and cannot deny himself, and he will not allow us to be tempted above what we can bear, but he makes a way of escape for us in that temptation. It means that everything we go through is common to man and we can bear it; otherwise, he will not allow it to come to us.

It will be rewarding to see what the Scripture further says about divorce in 1 Corinthians 7: 10.

> ***'And unto the married I command, yet not I but the lord, let not the wife depart from her husband: but and if she depart, let her remain unmarried or be reconciled back to her husband: and let not the husband depart from his wife.'***

Unity and oneness or togetherness is a prerequisite for a happy marriage. When a woman leaves her home for whatever reason, she has broken fellowship with her husband and vice versa. The Bible commands that we do not separate from our spouses, and if we do, we should remain unmarried or go back. The Scripture is clear; there is no confusion of what the Spirit of God is saying in regards to divorce.

A man is required to forgive, ask of God the grace to forgive the one that has offended you. As children of God, we know the mind of our Father; he has revealed his will through his word. His word says that he hates divorce. Malachi 2: 15-16 says:

> *'And did not God make you and your wife one flesh? Did not one make you and preserve your spirit alive? And why did God make you two one? Because he sought a godly offspring from your union. Therefore take heed to yourselves, and let no one deal treacherously and be faithless to the wife of his youth. For the lord, the God of Israel says: I hate divorce and marital separation and he who covers his garment his wife with violence. Therefore keep a watch upon your spirit that it may be controlled by my spirit that you deal not treacherously and faithlessly with your marriage mate.'*
> Amplified version.

Some have the habit of physically and verbally abusing their wives; God hates that. If you have been hurt deeply by your spouse and you feel that you can't carry on any longer, I will advice that you look back to what Jesus said. 'Pray for those who hurt you,' he said. The secret in praying for the one that hurt you is that, as you pray for them, healing comes to your heart through your sincere prayers. I'm not talking about prayers for vengeance, but a selfless prayer of love. Most people I have counselled admit that they find it difficult to pray for their spouses who have hurt them. It is so because they allow their bitter experiences to dominate their thoughts and actions. Allow the Word of God to dominate your mind instead. The devil also will not make it easy for you to pray for your spouse; he'll rather amplify the issues showing you how unfairly you've been treated, refuse to look at the pictures that the devil wants you to see. Decide to pray for your spouse; once you do, you have journeyed into the way of victory.

I remember a time in my life when I felt terribly hurt, and everything in me was screaming for a divorce. I thought having a divorce was the only way out of my dilemma. I knew life was never going to be the same for me once I get a divorce, but I wanted it anyhow. My healing came one day, in the shower, as I listened to that inward anointing that teaches you all things. I listened as he began to pray through me. Before long, I was in tears praying out the will of God for my marriage as I heard him pray; all the walls of unforgiveness were broken down, and there I was weeping. He sees our hearts and feels our pains. I felt like he was saying 'it's okay'. I felt his love wrapped around me, and I was comforted, and after that day, I realised that I was healed of all my pains. There were times when I would deliberately look for the pain in my heart by being resentful, but the pain had gone; it wasn't there, Jesus had taken them all away. Only God's love has the ability to heal your pains. Hallelujah.

I would challenge anybody who is born again and is willing to yield their will for God's will; the Spirit of God will help you to see these truths that I share with you. He will confirm his word. Things have changed in marriages today because of a zero-percent tolerance. This is nothing that we have ever seen; the end of all things is near and the king is coming very soon, and so the devil is working overtime to deceive people. He is running to and fro seeking whom he may devour. The Bible says that if it were possible, even the very elect will be deceived (Matt. 24: 24). But God will do a quick work and cut it short in righteousness (Rom. 9: 28). So that there will be a remnant; the vessels of mercy.

The Antidote of Divorce

When Jesus preached in Nazareth, Bible says he could not do any miracles there because of their unbelief. So he went into the temple and began to teach them. He knew that if he could help them to understand the Scriptures, their understanding will produce faith that will cause them to get healed.

The antidote for divorce is proper teaching of God's Word. If people could go to college full time for three to four years to educate themselves just so they could find a befitting job, then we should learn about marriage longer than we do now because marriage is meant to last for lifetime. The announcement of a couple's intention to get married should be made after they have undergone an extensive marriage course. I pray that these marriage courses will be introduced in every church just as we have new converts class and baptismal classes. The ideal duration should be twice a week for at least one year for those intending to get married. We could also start teachings about marriage as a preparatory class in our youth meetings. The church must do all in its power to eradicate this problem of divorce that eats so deep in our flesh today.

Prayer

Lord, you are the father of all flesh and God of all creation. The word of your mouth is truth. You are the architect of marriage and you designed it to last forever. Divorce has never been a part of your idea. Help me lord to please you in my marriage, even in the face of oppositions. I must forgive every wrong done to me by my spouse so that the enemy will not come in and put asunder what you have joined together. I have realized that my true happiness comes from you alone. May my love for my spouse be perfected in Christ in Jesus name. Amen

Chapter Nine

The Devastating Effects of Divorce

The effects of divorce far outweigh the problems that people are running away from. It has a tremendous effect on the children, especially if they are still very young during the divorce. I have had adults tell me how badly hurt and empty they felt as kids when their parents separated. I'm sure that parents have very little knowledge about what extend their decisions and actions affect the children and for how long the effect is felt. Most children assume that the outgoing parent was kicked out of the house, so they blame the other parent for causing all the trouble. Some find it hard to keep long-lasting relationships because of the fear that their spouse may want to leave them, or that their marriage might end up like their parents'. Some end up treating their spouses just as they saw their parents treating each other. Yet others no longer believe in long-term relationships. For some, the insecurity and fear of losing the other parent after the divorce is tormenting and has led many into using drugs and sex. I heard about a fourteen-year-old-girl who lived with her dad and her stepmother. She had been broken once when her parents divorced. And now she lost her dad to cancer and had difficulties coming out of her loss. The insecurity and loneliness she felt drove her into the sex game. She began to have sex uncontrollably; she finally got pregnant three months after her dad died. Although it wasn't her fault that her dad died, but it just shows how far this feeling of insecurity and rejection can take a child. Separation from a parent or both parents surely has a destructive ability in the life of a child; it does not matter if the cause of the separation is death or divorce.

One common effect of divorce is that it deprives children from learning, and also receiving love from the outgoing parent. It's been said that teenage daughters tend towards their fathers, but if the father is no longer in the home, they are tempted to fill that void with other males elsewhere. Sex and prostitution becomes their consolation. Some children become resentful, blaming one parent for causing the divorce. It is difficult for a mother to raise sons without their father, the head of the family; it only takes the grace of God to bring them upright. It is also difficult for fathers to take care of daughters without their mother. There has to be a balance in the family. If these children are introduced to the Holy Spirit, who is the father of all, he will fill up every gap in their hearts.

For the couple, divorce could make them very unforgiving and bitter, especially if their expectations after the divorce fail to happen. Some will use the children as a tool to ill-treat the other. Unforgiveness, bitterness, and resentments are weapons that the enemy uses to deprive Christians from experiencing God's blessings. It is very unhealthy for one to go into a second relationship; carrying such baggage and without first dealing with the issues that broke the first marriage because if that happens, what caused the first one to break will also cause the second one to break. The healing process begins when we lay ourselves bare before the Lord and allow him to show us what actually went wrong; the supposed cause of the divorce is actually signs of the main problem manifesting itself. For example, if the cause of the divorce is infidelity, that infidelity is a sign of dissatisfaction of some sort. So the dissatisfaction which is the actual problem has led to infidelity. People need to understand that no one could actually satisfy a person. They may try their best to make amends in areas of their lives where they feel their spouses are not happy about, but soon after that change another area that displeases may surface. Only God can satisfy a person. Trust the Spirit of God to help feel the void in your life.

The effect of divorce also clings on the finances of the individuals. Bills they both pay together now become one person's responsibility. The struggle to be updated with all the bills could drive the individual deeper into depression. The new budget might not be sufficient to give the children the kind of fun they used to have. Holidays and recreational activities might be cut out for some time.

Psychological effect that divorce has on individual comes in diverse manners. The individual could experience a lack of interest in domestic and social activities. Many will find it difficult to open themselves up for new relationships. It's not just them not wanting an intimate relationship, but any other kinds of relationships as well. They may become critical of everyone, and also judgemental. They may think that everyone wants to take advantage of them, and as a result, they raise up their 'protective banners' each time a person tries comes into their lives.

Divorce also has an effect on the body of Christ. It encourages younger believers to use the exit door if challenges to their marriages seem intolerable to them. It can bring about so many hurting people in the church, including children. It undermines God's order for the family. The fear and insecurity deprives affected Christians from spreading the Gospel as they should. A believer who had a divorce may find it difficult to preach against it, or persuade someone else not to.

If you are already divorced, don't condemn yourself; don't blame yourself for what has happened because without the Holy Spirit it is impossible for you to do right, and that is why he came. Like the Apostle Paul said in Philippians 3: 13-14.

> *'. . . Forgetting those things which are behind and reaching forth unto those things which are before.'*

Press forward the mark for the prize of the high calling of God in Christ Jesus that you may apprehend that for which you are apprehended. God's purpose for your life will still come to pass as you go to him in complete surrender. You can still be who he wants you to be, just rest in his love. Refuse to let the past control your future. Forgive the one that had brought this pain to your heart and wake up to a new day with God. The devil might sometimes bring accusations and guilt against you for the primary purpose of making you live in self-condemnation; I want to remind you that Christ is your warrant against every accusation of the enemy. These accusations might come in different ways, don't succumb to them; just as a police officer will lift up his warrant to make an arrest, so you should lift up Christ in your heart. Remember, a police officer's warrant silences every argument; it commands compliance. So it is when you lift up Christ as your warrant, the devil will have nothing more to say but to flee. Christ is your defence. See 1 Corinthians 1: 5, amplified version.

God's plan for your life is to give you a future and a hope, to bring you to an expected end. What is your expected end? I believe your expected end is that you want to finish well. God's plan is to help you finish well. Apostle said he had fought a good fight and finished his course. He is actually declaring that he had come to his expected end through faith in God. And I declare in the name of Jesus that you will be all that he has purposed for you to be as you yield your will for his.

Prayer

Dear father, you are the God who upholds all things by the word of your power. Your plans towards us are for good, to bring us to an expected end but the plan of the enemy is to frustrate us and hurt our children. I pray thee, that as many of us that have been touched by the effect of this grievous mistake called divorce, that your mercy will prevail and bring healing to our souls.

I pray that the eyes of the church be opened to see what we are doing to ourselves and repent of it. I trust that your spirit who runs the church will do the work. Thank you for your mercies in Jesus name. Amen

Chapter Ten

Mending a Broken Marriage

I read of a story in the ministry of a preacher who has long gone to be with the Lord, Smith Wigglesworth. He told about a man whose wife cheated on him, left him, and went to be with this other man. He was so bitter that one day he decided to take his wife's life. He got a knife under his sleeves and headed off. That same day, Mr Wigglesworth was having an open-air meeting in the area; he realised that this man had been hanging around even after the meeting; he walked up to him and began preaching to him. That same night the man confessed his sins weeping, and received salvation. Jesus got into him and made him a changed man. He forgave his wife, got himself together, got a new home, and invited his wife back home. She came back to him soberly and received salvation too. Our Jesus is master in mending broken marriages.

Though this man felt pain and bitterness towards his wife, but as the Word of God got to him, he repented, realising his wrong before God. Though his bitterness was justified yet God's love required that he forgives. Like we discussed in earlier chapters, only a proud heart will refuse to forgive. When God reveals himself to a person, he fills you with so much love like nothing you've ever experienced. That divine influence over your life changes you. John, the writer of the book of Revelation said, 'And when I saw him, I fell at his feet as dead'.

His presence in your life kills everything that is contrary to him. We must all crave to have a revelation of this Prince of life, Jesus.

The man in Mr Wigglesworth story was not defensive as he heard the Word of God. He opened up his spirit that he may receive. Self-defence is another weapon the devil uses to blindfold people. When a person is always defensive of their actions, they fail to see the picture that God wants to show them. Such people have built walls around them so high that the word cannot have a free flow into their spirits. God sees that injustice that has been done against you, and that is why he wants to fix things for you. He is your defence.

Dearly beloved, there is no marriage that God cannot fix, nothing is impossible for God to do, no one is so bad and wicked that God cannot change. He is not willing to give up even on a murderer. It is not his will that any should perish but all to come to repentance, his desire is for your spouse to be saved. God can mend your marriage that has been broken for five years if only you will believe. It doesn't matter if there was violence before the separation, God can still fix it. Remember the Apostle Paul who persecuted the early church, he took delight in killing anyone who confesses Christ. But when God took a hold of him, Paul became a changed man. He that once persecuted the church became the apostle of that very message that he was against. Praise God.

Bible says if a woman leaves or divorces her husband, she must remain unmarried or return back to her husband lest she be an adulteress, and anyone who marries her commits adultery. This Scripture is in the New Testament, yet many have ignored it and have decided to do things their own way. The Scriptures cannot be broken. We cannot interpret the Scriptures to suit us because they are not for any personal interpretation.

God's will is for us to forgive our spouses and return home. Jesus said, if you love me, you will keep my words. Our love for the master is expressed when we deny ourselves and yield our will for his. Your love for Christ must be greater than your pride; it must be greater than your sufferings. When you suffer persecutions in your marriage, you are actually partaking in the fellowship of his suffering because it is the seed of God in you that the enemy seeks to destroy. In Philippians 2: 10, Paul declares thus:

> *'For my determined purpose is that I may know him, that I may progressively become more deeply and intimately acquainted with him, perceiving and recognizing and understanding the wonders of his person more strongly and more clearly, and that i may in that same way come to know the power outflowing from his resurrection which it exerts over believers, and that i may so share his sufferings as to be continually transformed in spirit into his likeness even to his death.'* amplified version.

This statement is one of the most profound statements in the Bible. This kind of knowing can only come through revelation. If we know Jesus in this manner, everything we go through becomes small. You will be ready to give up all for Jesus.

You may have been touched by the Spirit of God and you want to start all over again with your spouse, you can do it, not by your own strength, but by the strength that comes from God's Word.

But first you must look into your lives individually through the mirror of God and make changes as he shows you, as you keep digesting the word, it transforms you.

If you and your spouse are Christians and you got divorced, I trust that the Holy Spirit has began his work in you; confess your faults one to the other and forgive all the wrong that you have suffered for the sake of your love for the lord Jesus. His will is for you to be reunited with your spouse. If you let him, he will make all things beautiful and new. He will turn your shame into beauty and your tears into joy. Remember, as you go back home, go in Jesus' name; no more anger, no resentments, and no feelings of guilt because all things have become new. And the peace of God, which passes all understanding, shall keep your hearts and minds through Christ Jesus. Amen.

Prayer

Heavenly father, the one to whom nothing is impossible. I believe you can fix my broken marriage if I am willing to surrender my all to you. Thank you for giving me the privilege of being re-united back with my spouse. Help me lord, to throw away all bitterness and resentment so that I can see what you are showing me. I receive the truth of your word with humbleness of mind, and as I re-unite with my spouse, may my shame be turned into beauty. I reject the spirit of pride and welcome the Holy Spirit into my life in Jesus name. Amen

Chapter Eleven

Embrace the Prince of Peace

You cannot successfully be married to your spouse without you first marrying to our Lord Jesus. We are his bride and he is our bridegroom. When your spiritual marriage is not right, your physical marriage will not be right too. If you are tired and frustrated in trying to make your marriage work, then hear the words of the master, he is calling you. He said, 'Come unto me all ye that labour and are heavy laden and I will give you rest.' What kind of rest is the master promising here? Notice, he said, 'I will give you.' It therefore means that you cannot get it yourself; it is something that only divinity can offer. Rest is a place of refreshing, a place of tranquillity. It is a freedom from struggle and turmoil. Only Christ can give this kind of rest, and he is willing. All you need to do is, come.

If you are reading this book and you are at the verge of a divorce, I want you to know that nothing is difficult for him of whom all things consist. It is not about what he can do but what you can believe. Embrace him like a child that sees danger and runs into the arms of the mother. Now you know his word concerning divorce, you now know it does not please your heavenly Father. Repent from that thought and decide today to honour God in your marriage and God Almighty will be your exceeding great reward.

If you are already divorced, don't live in self-condemnation. The acknowledgement of wrong is the beginning of repentance. Talk to the Lord and command his blessings at the point where you're at. When Father Abraham went against God's will and had Ishmael, he repented before God and asked God to bless Ishmael. Now Ishmael was Abraham's mistake, and God, gracious in mercy answered that prayer. God did not show us his love because we did right; He showed us love in our wrong. What an unconditional love! Therefore, there is hope for you. Christ is the repairer of life. If you trust him, he will restore your life back, cause his goodness to shine on you and make you happy again.

If you are reading this book and you are not yet born again, I encourage you to open your heart to Jesus and receive the grace of God. All the graces of God can only be available to you if you receive him. Jesus said unless you are born again you cannot enter the kingdom of God. You have to be in the kingdom first before accessing the goodies in it. Remember, the price of your sins have been paid in full on the cross where Jesus died. If you reject Jesus, you are literally saying you don't want his sacrifice for your sins, and you want to pay for your sins yourself. Why don't you accept his sacrifice and allow his love to reign in you by saying this simple but most powerful prayer:

Dear Father, I come to you in the name of Jesus. Your word says if I confess with my mouth the Lord Jesus, and believe in my heart that God has raised him from the dead, I shall be saved. I declare the lordship of Jesus in my life, and I believe in my heart that you raised him from the dead. I declare that I'm saved, I am born again.

I now live the rest of my life for the one who loves me and gave himself for me. Thank you, Father, in Jesus name I pray. Amen.

If you said this prayer, welcome to God's family. You are now a new creation in Christ. Begin to feed your spirit with the word. Join a local church around you and experience God's grace. God bless you.

Let us know how this book has been a blessing to you. Email us at: *info@thenewcreation.com*. We like to hear your testimonies and rejoice with you.

Frequently Asked Questions

I have been trying hard to show love to my wife but she just does not want to recognise my effort, do I quit or what?

In marriage we don't quit. Stop trying to love her just love her unconditionally. It is your responsibility according to Ephesians 5:23 to love your wife, just as Christ loves the church patiently washing her with the word. I would advice that you spend more time building your relationship with Jesus through prayers and the study of God's word, as you do your wife will be drawn to the light in you.

My husband and I are Christians but we are not happy in our marriage because a lot had gone wrong in the past, things don't seem good at the moment. What do I do?

Dear sister, the only way to be happy again is to forgive one another and to put that painful past behind you. James 5:16 says confess your faults one to another and pray for one another that you may be healed. As long as you keep talking about those issues, you will keep getting hurt afresh. If God forgives us our sins we ought also to forgive one another. you cannot serve God genuinely with unforgiveness in your hearts. The enemy has used these problems as an occasion to steal the joy in your marriage. Spend time in the word by getting out all the scriptures that talks about forgiveness and meditate on them, your healing will spring up.

Is it ok for a Christian to marry a non Christian? My brother is about to get married to a non Christian, we have spoken to him but he would not listen.

God has put certain principles in place for our own good. Marriage is a life time commitment; we can only succeed by doing the word. Our failure to obey is the reason for the divorce 2 Corinthians 6:14 quotes, be ye not unequally yoked together with unbelievers: for what fellowship hath righteousness with unrighteousness? And what communion hath light with darkness? Now we all know that though a cat and a dog may dwell together, yet it is unnatural for them to assimilate together, in the same vein a Christian and a non Christian can work together but cannot marry. Bible says in the mouth of two or three witnesses a matter is established, so if we look back to the Old Testament we will find out that God commanded the Israelites not to marry foreigners and in the book of Ezra they were asked to put away their foreign wives. The reason is that these unbelieving ones will influence us and weaken our faith. Just the way those women introduced their foreign gods to the Israelites. So if your brother is completely yielded to the word of God, he will listen to the voice of the word.

My fiancé always asks me for sex, would it be wrong since we are going to get married?

You do not want to start a relationship on a wrong note. Sex before marriage is sin. The bible calls it fornication, and it is God's will that we abstain from fornication. Again, abstinence is not denial, just wait and get married first. 1 Thessalonians 4:3 says, "for this is the will of God, even your sanctification, that you should abstain from fornication: that every one of you should know how to posses his vessel in sanctification and honour". There are several scriptures in the bible that warns the believer against fornication, example, jude 1:7, revelation 2:20, 1 corinthians 7:1-2, and so on. Your fiancé must learn to subject his flesh under the authority of the spirit of God. Romans 8:13 says, "for if ye live after the flesh, ye shall die: but if ye through the spirit do mortify the deeds of the body, ye shall live".

Why is there a change in the way a man loves his wife during courtship and after marriage?

You are not really specific in your question, but a man ought to love his wife even more than when he was courting her. Love and care is what he owes his wife, so if he fails to perform his duties towards her, he has not only failed her but failed God. If he ill-treats his wife, he ill-treats himself, so says the word. Ephesians 5:28, "so ought men to love their wives as their own bodies. He that loveth his wife loveth himself".

Why are there so many divorced Christians in the church even though the bible teaches against it?

As the days get darker, each one of us must work out our salvation with fear and trembling. God said in Acts 17:30, "and the times of ignorance God overlooked but now command all men everywhere to repent". It is clearly written in the bible that God hates divorce and Jesus also explained that it was permitted in the law of Moses because of the hardness of man's heart. We have heard it from the saviour himself so why do Christians still do it? It is either that most churches are not teaching against it because some of the teachers themselves are guilty of it, or many go ahead and do it because they say it will not affect their salvation. But Jesus said in Mathew 7:21, "not everyone who says to me "lord, lord" shall enter the kingdom of heaven, but he who does the will of my father in heaven". John said in 1 john 2:4, "he that saith I know him and keepeth not his commandments, is a liar, and the truth is not in him."

If once saved is always saved no matter what they do, then why does the bible warn against backsliding and apostasy? There is a lot of deception out there but the words of God are our sure guide, we must live by his word.

Could you please throw more light on the issue of Christian re-marriage, I have been divorced for some years but before my divorce I knew very little about the bible, I'm now considering re-marrying, will I be sinning?

My dear, these are questions that must people see as difficult to answer, but we must not go by feeling only by the word. 1 corinthians 7:10-11, "And unto the married i command, yet not i, but the lord, let not the wife depart from her husband: but and if she depart, let her remain unmarried, or be reconciled to her husband: and let not the husband put away his wife". According to the bible, the only time a woman is free to re-marry to someone else is if her husband dies. So if your ex-husband is still alive and unmarried, the word of God is encouraging you to go back to him. Now, it is essential that you pray for his salvation if he is not saved, and you too must unreservedly give yourself to the lord. You could get your pastor involved in this prayer exercise; if you do, the lord will surely honour you for honouring his word. If you were not a born again before your divorce, don't condemn yourself, no one can do right without the leading of God's Spirit. At any point that one realizes that they have sinned against God and repents of that sin, the bible says he is faithful and just to forgive and to cleanse us from all unrighteousness. As you give your life to Christ, you are a new creature, old things have passed away and all things have become new, 2corinthians 5:17.

I am thinking of getting married but the woman that I'm considering is divorced, will i be wrong to marry her?

It actually depends on the circumstance surrounding her divorce. The bible teaches that she gets back with her husband or remain unmarried. The only exception in the bible is if her husband dies. But if he is alive and already married to someone else, what you should do is to listen prayerfully to what the Holy Spirit will say to you. Bible says it is better for a person to be married than to burn with passion.

My husband disagrees with me each time I asked him to tithe. He believes that whatever he gives for an offering covers for tithe. Please what is the truth?

Your question is interesting, tithing is another major topic of debate in the church, some say it is under the law and in the New Testament believers do not have to tithe. The truth about tithing has been glaring in the bible but not seen by many. Though we are no longer under the law but under grace, tithing came before the law, it pre-existed the law. The law came by Moses but Abraham who lived many generations before Moses paid tithe to the king of Salem. As Christians, we give our tithes as an act of obedience to God's word. An offering is different from tithe. You can choose whatever amount you want to give for offering but your tithe is fixed, the bible says ten percent of your income. So tithes and offerings are two different types of giving.

Mary, I just found out that my husband has been cheating with my friend, I am so hurt, I don't think I can continue any longer.

Is your husband a born again Christian? Well if he is not, the first thing is to get him saved. I can understand your pain and frustration, and you are justified to feel this way but I want you to know that though he had done wrong he may not necessarily be a bad man. Will you throw away your marriage for this? If he has repented and apologised please find it in your heart to forgive him and receive him back for the sake of Jesus. God by himself will take the pain off you if you do. As the woman you must save your marriage, begin to pray for your marriage so that the enemy does not bring in something worse.

My question is this, there are two gentle men in my life and they both want to marry me, I love them both and I don't know which one to choose.

The answer to your question lies within you. You must first be sure that the one you eventually choose is a born again Christian, secondly, don't rush to get married because once you go in you cannot come out, it is a must that you and the one you choose attend sound marriage counselling classes. To help you decide, get to know each one of them and find out with which of them you are most comfortable, who do you feel more at home with. Above all, pray for God's guidance in making the right decision.

I and my wife never seem to agree on anything, the arguments are endless, do you think we can still make a successful marriage?

As Christians you must live a life free from strive. You are the head of the home so you must find out what actually causes these arguments and why. The word of God covers every area of our lives so go to the word and find out what it says about your issues. You know it takes two to tangle, if you do not indulge in those arguments they will not hold water. A good manager does not argue with employees when problems arise, rather he explains things patiently to them. Be gentle with your wife and explain things in love. I recommend you study the chapter five and seven of this book carefully, it will make you understand who you are and how you should handle challenges in your marriage.

Is it right for married couples to live apart from each other, my best friend and her husband live in different countries, though he visits her twice in the year it still does not feel right.

It is not right for couples to live apart though some may do it because they found employment someplace else. God's purpose for marriage is for companionship. The bible teaches that we do not stay away from each other in all sense except for the purpose of prayer so that we may not be tempted by the devil. Staying away from your spouse for too long may lead to adultery which will eventually destroy the family. I do not know for what reason your friends live apart but anything that does not create allowance for the family is not worth considering. If a proposed job abroad will not allow a man to take his family along eventually, then it should not be taken. The family is more important.

The bible says a man should leave his father and mother and cleave to his wife, what does this mean?

Well it simply means that the man comes out of his own family for the purpose of starting a new one. It does not imply that he abandons his own parents but he is now committed to his own wife, all his attention should be on his own. One of the meaning of the Hebrew word translated 'cleave' means to pursue hard after someone else. A man ought to pursue hard after his wife so much that there is no other person he is this close to. However, his parents are to be honoured.

What do I do, my husband has refused to get a job like everyone else. He stays home every day watching TV while I go to work. I am tired of living with him like this.

I understand your frustration because there has been a displacement of roles. But you know there are some men who prefer working for themselves than getting a regular job. Have you tried to find out if he would like to do something on his own? Remember, you are in his life to help him, you know his strengths and weaknesses, talk to him with love, encourage him without been critical, he may need to understand that the word of God says he is the head of the home. Pray for him sincerely and continue to show him love. May the lord strengthen you. You did not say whether he is born again or not. If he is not born again, he needs Christ in his life. “Bible says a man who does not provide for his own household is worse than an infidel.”

Index

N

O

P

S

T

U

V

W

Lightning Source UK Ltd.
Milton Keynes UK
03 December 2010

163850UK00001B/20/P